More praise for *Post-Volcanic Folk Tales*

"This ferocious debut reads like no other. Where grief and exuberance dance under an encauldroned blood moon, mellifluous pyrotechnic *incantatas* hurl cacophonous fissile sparks, the unsung summoned into being. I am astounded by the invention and necessity of Mackenzie Polonyi's mutating forms, multigenerational matriarchy writ mythically large and tragically precise in the wide wake of displacement."

—Timothy Liu, author of *Down Low and Lowdown*

"This formally restless—indeed, volcanic—collection disgorges poems of testimony and supplication, unsettling yet embodied, mercurial yet real. Ravenously, Mackenzie Polonyi embraces her maternal genealogy, transforming tragic histories of violence into a lyrical lament of immense linguistic intensity. This is poetry that turns lack into excess, elegy into a procession of alchemical adjectives, pain into a fever of the figurative. Opening this book is akin to entering a butcher shop where a girl-child—'raised secondhand homesick'—has been hoarding her grief between sugared milk and vinegar. Her rebellion against speechlessness is mounting page after page: 'The history of a daughter is growing a garden of blood for a wound with a stomach of air that will swallow time like a mirror.'"

—Valzhyna Mort, author of *Music for the Dead and Resurrected*

"In Mackenzie Polonyi's stunning debut collection, the human body becomes a landscape inscribed by multigenerational story, memory, and trauma. In these visceral lyric poems, boundaries between self and nature dissolve. Polonyi unearths ancestral connections—'stone ruins cob-webbing my sternum'—as her symptoms and injuries merge with her suspended yet rooted foremothers' own ruptures. An alchemical blend of folklore and science preserves rituals like 'pigeon-milk' tonics amid seismic turbulence, propelling Polonyi's searing language. Wonderfully kaleidoscopic in its exploration of a scattered and often uncertain identity, this book transports readers into realms where memories ossify into 'rusted peafowl-blue' relics. Blistering yet nurturing, *Post-Volcanic Folk Tales* reckons with how inherited psychic and corporeal complexities ultimately give rise to a profoundly compassionate yet questioning devotion, revealing: 'my hands / they are becoming your hands' across endless loss and regeneration. Look out! This book will change you."

—Christopher Salerno, author of *The Man Grave*

POST-VOLCANIC FOLK TALES

MACKENZIE POLONYI

NATIONAL POETRY SERIES WINNER
SELECTED BY ISHION HUTCHINSON

BROOKLYN, NEW YORK

The National Poetry Series congratulates the five winners
of the 2023 National Poetry Series competition:

Field Guide for Accidents by Albert Abonado
Chosen by Mahogany L. Browne for Beacon Press

Post-Volcanic Folk Tales by Mackenzie Polonyi
Chosen by Ishion Hutchinson for Akashic Books

The Sky Was Once a Dark Blanket by Kinsale Drake
Chosen by Jacqueline Trimble for University of Georgia Press

Transgenesis by Ava Nathaniel Winter
Chosen by Sean Hill for Milkweed Editions

the space between men by Mia S. Willis
Chosen by Morgan Parker for Penguin

♦

THE
NATIONAL
POETRY
SERIES

♦

*The National Poetry Series was established in 1978 to ensure the publication
of five collections of poetry annually through five participating publishers.
The Series has been funded over the years by Amazon Literary Partnership,
the Gettinger Family Foundation, Bruce Gibney, HarperCollins Publishers,
the Stephen and Tabitha King Foundation, Lannan Foundation, Newman's
Own Foundation, Anna and Olafur Olafsson, Penguin Random House, the
Poetry Foundation, Hawthornden Foundation, Elise and Steven Trulaske,
and the National Poetry Series Board of Directors.*

————

All rights reserved. No part of this book may be reproduced, stored in a retrieval system, or transmitted in any form, by any means, including mechanical, electronic, photocopying, recording, or otherwise, without the prior written consent of the publisher.

Published by Akashic Books
©2024 Mackenzie Polonyi

ISBN: 978-1-63614-196-1
Library of Congress Control Number: 2024936199

All rights reserved
First printing

Akashic Books
Brooklyn, New York
Instagram, X, Facebook: AkashicBooks
info@akashicbooks.com
www.akashicbooks.com

FOR ÉDES NAGYMAMÁM,
NANA, MY BELOVED SECOND MOTHER,
MY HUNGARIAN REFUGEE.

MINDIG IGAZ SZERETETTEL. MILLIÓ PUSZI.

FOR ŐSAKÁCFÁIM, MY FORROBINIEAEMOTHERS,
TENDERS OF APRICOTS TENDERS OF GRAPES.

FOR DIASPORIC DAUGHTERS, MEDICAL MYSTERIES,
AND IDENTIFIED PATIENTS.

DRÁGA NAGYPAPÁM: I RECEIVED YOUR SPIRIT OF RESISTANCE
AND YOUR TŰZ.

EVERY ANGEL IS TERRIFYING.
—Rainer Maria Rilke

AS WE RESIST THE PAST WE BEGIN TO QUESTION THE GRIEF WE WIELD AS
ASH ACROSS OUR FACES.
—Layli Long Soldier

IF YOU HAVE A DEEP SCAR, THAT IS A DOOR.
IF YOU HAVE AN OLD, OLD STORY, THAT IS A DOOR.
IF YOU LOVE THE SKY AND THE WATER SO MUCH YOU ALMOST CANNOT
BEAR IT, THAT IS A DOOR.
—Clarissa Pinkola Estés

BUT THE DEFINITION OF *MYTH* IS *NOUN*,
THE IDEA THAT ANY ONE CREATURE CAN EVER HEAR ANOTHER.
—Sumita Chakraborty

Contents

The opening line of Mackenzie Polonyi's *Post-Volcanic Folk Tales* alerts us to metamorphosis. It stands by itself above a cluster of lines, and this isolation gives it a particular oracular weight, which is the burden, both load and song, we encounter to different degrees throughout. The line seems taken from an ongoing story into which we are dropped without knowledge of the current stage of transformation. Even more frightening, the first clause indicates that the transformation might not be change but duplication, a circular delirium without advancement. Yet, the rational tone makes us trust the voice's authority; it convinces us that the strange, arresting detail of the second clause is nothing but a memory of a lived experience. The line reads in full:

> In one version of the story, you inherit acidic rain like genetic instructions.
> ("Gingerbread")

The voice strikes like a kind of latter-day Scheherazade's, creating her own small counternarratives betwixt larger hegemonic ones that serve only to confine her and her foremothers to the unchangeable law of hereditary weakness and suffering, rather than to their transformational power to survive.

Toward the end of the poem, this Scheherazade figure declares that the elemental properties of the earth are her tools to create these counternarratives of self. She says, "I am made of stone, mud, bark, believe me, dare believe me." Throughout the collection, we hear this plea in different guises. It is there in the shape of irony, grief, anger, and joy, and often of all of these combined, testifying to the speaker's existence against existential threats.

Claiming those simple matters for herself, the poet-storyteller undergoes forms of difficult, grotesque, even humiliating procedures so as not to become engulfed by the gatekeepers' telling of history. The frail body battling illnesses brutally real and psychosomatic withstand and repel these traumas, often through regurgitation, a theme the final section of "Gingerbread" sets into motion:

> In the last version of the story, you are cradled like a cave in the palm of death on a
> yellow tram line.
> You become pyretic from temperature dysregulation.

You vomit aragonite and flowers of iron yet you are still unbelievable.
A single raven-faced angel places a kiss of frozen water upon your forehead.
The compass of your spine now demagnetized.
Vision is a vortex of poppy seed in steaming milk.

[...]

A physician points an accusative finger: STORYTELLER!

You regurgitate a skeleton key shiny with bile.
Its bow—proof—is shaped like the rift lake of a hoof.

By the time we get to "Butcher Shop Rendezvous," a splendid, harrowing prose poem in the center of the collection, we realize that vomiting is a way for the body to rebel against not only the imposing figure of the physician but all authoritarian figures who seek to keep the body in check. Regurgitating, then, is a form of vivid confession. Here are two increasingly graphic instances in "Butcher Shop Rendezvous" of that rebelling throat:

We tap grey throats of patrilineal beech-dolls for sap, smear beards and handlebar mustaches on father-photographs with half-truth grease, drink our bull's blood by crystal decanters then lengthily vomit woodchips of broken promises.

[...]

A Sapphic lavender-violet wreath upon my head, I was raised hungry, flea-hearted, hypoglycemic, often hairless in peach-sized patches, lapping up spiral galaxy breast milk in the rose-bloom wombs of my dreams, my urethra burning like vomit, my bladder diseased, inflamed, scarred, and popping, I was urine-marking everything, all ketones and albumin, leaving behind my very own feral scent so I could recognize myself later on, pawing at clots of false hope which hung from glistening butcher hooks like my favorite egg noodle dumplings.

In an earlier poem, "The Shoemaker's Daughter," the rebellious throat appears first as a stony instrument resisting political invasion of her homeland:

When December's waxing crescent moon resembles a white pepper,
NAGYMAMA gets vacuumed back into occupied Hungary.
Sedative-Hypnotics gallop heavy-boned down her lithified throat,
bat-swatting her echolocative uvula with their rhythm-blue tails.

Toward the end of the poem, now displaced in America, the grandmother produces an enigmatic language for her granddaughter to decipher, a radial symmetry that informs the complex lyric of viscous lava coursing through these poems.

                                                                        She vomits
a stiff pigeon foot gripping a pinwheel bouquet of bile-wrinkled letters.
In our true future, I stick my hand through her arboreal urn
to place dragon meat beneath her withered tongue unlike a prescription drug.

These guttural moments of "a cry from throat to throat to throat" are everywhere in *Post-Volcanic Folk Tales*.

From oviparous throats, we throw truths about the buttercup
anemones of our bodies like live coals into one another's ear canals as if skip-
ping calcified stones. Our naveled mistakes, our electrochemical miscommunications
our volcanic violations, our proscribed pleasures inearthed unearthed: opal, snow-
drop, ox-eye, malachite, pheasant-eye, vesuvianite, vetch, efflorescent treasure. This
sharing—
a transgenerational brushing procession.
O umbilical chord of keratin, supply your nutrient-rich narrative.
("Doorways")

There again a plea refracts the buried elemental parts, what one poem calls "vertebral tectonics of memory," which surface from the density of a sanctioned national epic, to bear witness to the internal strength of the forgotten and the unacknowledged who most suffer the tyranny of political oppression. Of course, the majority of forgotten and unacknowl-edged victims are women. In poem after poem, we find Scheherazade in the painful act of retrieving the splinters of matrilineal memory. As such, each poem becomes its own archive, a veritable apparatus of truth and reconciliation in which the lost tales of women are atomized and preserved for the future. It is fatal, hard work. A beautiful passage expresses this conundrum:

> An earth-measurer moth, I have lost myself
> to the lantern of your ONCE. The moon of my future,
> my point of reference, my positive phototaxis,
> my navigational system, my nocturnal intelligence,
> all bewildered, all disrupted by the hypnotist of
> matriviticultural psychic inheritance swinging her pocket
> watch here, there. Before I witnessed
> my hands become plum, my grandmother's hands become snow,
> it was before I accordioned my body into her arboreal urn,
> eating off my very own ankles, wrists, limbs, sifting ossein.
> ("MOLTING IN THE MÁTRA MOUNTAINS")

This is the primary emotional terrain of *Post-Volcanic Folk Tales*. It is a fraught landscape in which an American granddaughter—we may risk calling her Scheherazade Polonyi—comes to terms with the progressive dementia and subsequent death of her Hungarian grandmother (stylized NAGYMAMA throughout), who was displaced from Hungary to New Jersey during the 1956 Hungarian Uprising.

Against this political backdrop, these complex, propulsive lyric sequences have the effect of lament or keening, hence the preponderance of the oracular vocative O in this collection.

> O tousled meanwhile of anonymity in which you glisten like a candle-kissed
> bloodhound—
> Here are my syllabic handkerchiefs gold-blossoming almost apparitional
> scents of citrus. Relocate our relation for I am bereft of you. Won't you unscatter
> your narrative from untraceable directions & harmonica yourself back?
> ("Estefelé / Toward Evening")

And again in the poem that immediately follows:

> O sunflower with your sugar equation,
> may I become your humble
> apprentice in synthesizing breath & water for growing

by an orchestra of light. Teach me your self-tending alchemy.
Or am I singing now of half-illusions?
O sunflower extracting radioactive contaminants from soil,
how I have rotated my own pseudanthium in solar devotion,
how I have rusted my stalk stuck & leaning
in NAGYMAMA's directionless direction.
("Phytoremediation (Ars Therapoetica)")

And later this funny, exquisite line from "MEGIDÉZNI ILONA DÉDNAGYNÉNI
SZELLEMÉT (A Staring Contest)": "Thus, I initiate our staring contest, O bright
ANCESTRESS!"

The device works like a tuning fork, lowering and heightening the emotional pitch
of poems that are not afraid to be vulnerable despite the real peril—public shaming,
ostracization—that comes with a culture that surveils the oviparous throats of women,
at times forbidding their voices from political discourse. No voice, no agency. In bold
defiance of that, "A Pogácsa Pantoum For Posthumous Love" ends with:

O BODILESSNESS O ENTANGLEMENT
O RESPLENDENT SILHOUETTE,
I forbid limits on the magic of love.

The astonished O of the vocative address—that "wooden O" Shakespeare calls "the
brightest heaven of invention" in *Henry V*—intensifies and draws attention. Polonyi is
deft at wielding a prosodic form of address reviled by contemporary poets as archaic and
ineffective into an anarchic weapon throughout *Post-Volcanic Folk Tales*. In several poems,
these Os show up contained in the gates of parenthesis. Hemmed in by oval walls, we
experience the astonished O as subtle sotto voce, an eerie soothsaying interjection, as
emphatic notice of something overlooked. The opening of "Sugar Geometry" is a resonant
instance:

opale-

scent (O her lard-stained apron unspooling

music of scaled tooth after scaled tooth;

a Balatonian school of tuning   forks!)

In NAGYMAMA's kávé   ring of melting pearls like a moon-

dial My small girl self again

in our former kitchen where withered umbilical cords

web beneath the floor

NAGYMAMA's teaspoon   silver uvula spelling O

skimming her teacup's scalloped mouth

(O—A gate I key with

the dragonflied tongue of my unfamiliar name)

Let's pause on that "dragonflied tongue." It is a good term for the Hungarian chan-
neled through the American English of a poet-storyteller-granddaughter who is not fluent
in the Hungarian of her maternal grandmother. Indeed, Polonyi achieves in *Post-Volcanic
Folk Tales* a third-space language through the same two steps of transcription and transla-
tion that genes take to make proteins.

Polonyi describes this process in "Piroska (Little Red Riding Hood)" as "vertically
vortexing." There is hardly a page in the collection where we don't find this form of vertical
vortexing—magmatic lines twisting layers of language into a red-hot core. But "Piroska
(Little Red Riding Hood)," a long, mostly prose poem sequence in the middle of the
collection is the supreme example of the dragonflied tongue set loose.

Piroska, as the poem's subheading makes clear, is the Hungarian name for the girl
in the fairytale. (The first syllable is certainly a play on *pyro*; she is a dangerous woman.)
Piroska becomes the granddaughter in this speculative narrative in which both factual and
fictive details move rapidly in multiple directions of time to chart the grandmother's trau-
matic experiences before and after the 1956 Hungarian Uprising. Undoubtedly, it is the
psychic pressure of these experiences, not to rule out a long history of familial illnesses,

which is part of the root cause of her dementia. Here, in full, is the moving penultimate section of the sequence. Note how it conveys another of Polonyi's gifts, that cumulative, incantatory drive of the anaphora, which enchants as much as it disenchants:

P corresponded, galloping fingers.

What big ears you have!
Milyen nagy füled van!

What big eyes you have!
Milyen nagy szemed van!

What big hands you have!
Milyen nagy kezed van!

What a horribly big mouth you have!
Milyen szörnyen nagy a szád!

A's ears big for listening forwards backwards obliquely vertically across vortexed calendars.
A's eyes big for visioning forwards backwards obliquely vertically across vortexed
    calendars.
A's hands big for reaching forwards backwards obliquely vertically across vortexed
    calendars.
A's mouth big for transmitting forwards backwards obliquely vertically across vor-
    texed calendars.

THE BIGGER A FERAL REFUGEE GROWS IN STORYTELLING OF THE
GYÜMÖLCSFÁK OF HOME,
THE SMALLER ÖRDÖGÖK OF POWER-MONEY-PROPAGANDA-GREED

Here, as well as elsewhere in the collection, Polonyi achieves a pyroclastic flow. Given how much ground she covers in order to honor her "matriviticultural psychic inheritance," this is no small feat. With unapologetic energy and verve, Mackenzie Polonyi inaugurates a sublime poetics of remembrance. *Post-Volcanic Folk Tales* is incendiary art, one strong enough to achieve the final transformation Polonyi prays for in these lines:

In my reverie, I heal
my women forwards backwards
of tank craters & venom
like horologium oscillatorium.
("Horologium Oscillatorium")

Ishion Hutchinson is the author of the poetry collections *School of Instructions, House of Lords and Commons*, and *Far District*. Born in Port Antonio, Jamaica, he is the W.E.B. Du Bois Professor in the Humanities at Cornell University.

Gingerbread

1

In one version of the story, you inherit acidic rain like genetic instructions.

You are a thatched roof enveiling a loam house within a feverish villineage.
It may be your biological defenses are kindling inflorescences of healthy tissue.
It may be your biological defenses are mistaking reed spears for spider nests.
The tears of the sky get uprooted like species of orchard weed by gravity-strong fingers.
The tears of the sky slope up a thatched roof spoon-silver like spittle or linen or a bed.
The tears of the sky puddle into platters that incandescent angel-faced ravens dance slow then fresh in.

Soon, you will crave the arrival of winter like citrus.

2

At noon, in another version of the story, you are a translucent girl burning with the karstic wolf of a virus.
Katicabogarak drink from lakes of melting mirrors while you sleep like a rocking horse.

You are a metronome knocking on the door of a mudbrick house.
You step accidentally into a platter of rain water.
The platter of rain water is a loaf of sweet bread.
The loaf of sweet bread is a buttercream drum cake.
The buttercream drum cake is a dunghill.
The dunghill, a cemetery.
The cemetery, a cry.

You somersault over and over and over into a wound with a voice like a season.
In a wound bridging another wound, you are a dream kissed inward against the wet-dry years of an older dream.
Tissue mouths sonorous storms into tissue.
Nest mouths treacherous music into nest.
At point of contact by wind, your living and phantom branches brush against, pressure into, bond, then pleach.

In wound time, one story like an earth casts its sun-bloodied shadow on the moon of another story.
Say syzygy backwards.
Say mézeskalácssütés.

3

In an alternative version of the story, a physician has forsaken your body in the forest of the word mystery.
There, you desiccate and shrink amidst lianas like ancient snakes.
Then, you hear a voice like vermillion ice in your right ear say the word miracle instead.
Sprouting out from your back, between your shoulder blades, is a pantograph.
Mother tongue is electrical power.

4

In the last version of the story, you are cradled like a cave in the palm of death on a yellow tram line.
You become pyretic from temperature dysregulation.
You vomit aragonite and flowers of iron yet you are still unbelievable.
A single raven-faced angel places a kiss of frozen water upon your forehead.
The compass of your spine now demagnetized.
Vision is a vortex of poppy seed in steaming milk.

You are a locust luminous with lichen twisted blue flames of bark plaited body nodding over a rock face.

Season after season, sewing needles feather and fishbone stitch your extremities.
You are hypotensive, hypoglycemic, pissing protein.
Your knuckles violet like ash; your nickname is corpse-hands!
Yet you are still unbelievable.

You say: my eyes my bladder my bones are burning acidic, grating like crows, throbbing like sky, swelling
like shadows, grinding like music, lightning is shooting and stretching and thistle-stinging all over the
meadow of my frame but primarily my femurs my calves my femurs, strong weed taproots are squeezing
and bruising like constricting ancient snakes, my bones my bladder my eyes are being gobbled up by a
wolf, ground by a pestle into hot sand, transposing themselves like musical keys, there is traffic in my
eyes my bladder my bones, each vehicle a blaring tooth, I am made of stone, mud, bark, believe me, dare
believe me.

A physician points an accusative finger: STORYTELLER!

You regurgitate a skeleton key shiny with bile.
Its bow—proof—is shaped like the rift lake of a hoof.

Doorways

Reflected in NAGYMAMA's portrait:
my mouth dilating vowels omphalic Ö Ö.
Two auroral doorways—
—The kitchen where she once
hand ground walnut, simmered
butcher's poppy in sugared milk, untun-
icked onion (our lachrymatory lily-mirror—), tenderized
meat. My only country. (—inside our fleshy
vegetal psychometric bulb I am a telephone
wire walker. For balance I grip an involuted uterine umbrella
whose ribs like an orbweaver's legs & spinnerets have wind-wilted by a temper from
a mountain cave deity hoarding rain clouds, hackles raised.)
—The mudroom. Slick liminal interval, transcen-
dental train terminal candlelit Keleti-yellow. A stopped shadow-
casting growth ring clock is our own secret
station's structural navel. A deciduous
tooth for a two way ticket!
The ticket inspector
deposits my mountainous molar into our dust-
encrusted genealogical bottle of Egri Bikavér,
& in exchange, returns my grape-infused forestial fang
gumward. Here: rainy shoeprints produce recursive puddle
illusions. Here: my dead demyelinating foremothers living
inflamed foremothers together
vinegar-pickling like vegetables in
the medicinal brine of Egerszalók Salt Hill Baths!
Masks of sunflower oil, egg yolk, sugar,
& black locust honey moisturizing exfoliating our storyfull foliose faces.
Masks of olive oil, egg white, curd,
& lemon bloodying our unblooming scalps,
the broom bristle ends of our bat roost hair.
Here: I study Ilona's arachnidian
hands relocating her twin acacia knights horizontally

vertically across our buoyant checkered board
like a pupil. DÉDNAGYNÉNI Ilona forms
an L for LISTEN! NEVER KILL A SPIDER! A movement
that wrinkles mineral water.
From oviparous throats, we throw truths about the buttercup
anemones of our bodies like live coals into one another's ear canals as if skip-
ping calcified stones. Our naveled mistakes, our electrochemical miscommunications
our volcanic violations, our proscribed pleasures inearthed unearthed: opal, snowdrop, ox-eye,
malachite, pheasant-eye, vesuvianite, vetch, efflorescent treasure. This sharing—
a transgenerational brushing procession.
O umbilical chord of keratin, supply your nutrient-rich narrative.

MEGIDÉZNI ILONA DÉDNAGYNÉNI SZELLEMÉT (A Staring Contest)

A portrait preserving the vernality of you
yellowing like leaf, linen, skin-split parchment,
varnished in prehistoric amber. The lustrous dusk of
negative space cradling you; sour water, amniotic, algaeic.
Negative space nacreous nectareous now
electrostatically forked by decades of touch. A spatiotemporal fracture.
Thus, I initiate our staring contest, O bright ANCESTRESS!
(A portrait is a portal is alluvial soil.)

        Out from one chalk-like
        moondial fault line—parting
        your hair's ceremonial rivulets,
        your hair's scrawling wildernesses,
        obsidian-rich & cinnamon-warm
        —let your spectral fingerbones bloom:

glacial italics, arthritic egrets wading
in my hippocampal wetlands. Floating heart, floating heart. Your dirt-
caked fingerbones play gossamer string games,
shaping broomsticks with strands of my hair, shaping stars
with my neural synapses. Your dirt-caked fingerbones shadow play
wolves upon warm wick-lit walls.

        The rectangle of your face; a viscerocranial aviary.
        Your pores like orchestral beaks, prismatic.
        An asymmetric cabinet of feathering
        collagenic ornaments, resemblance-prophetic.
        (A porcelain slipper-shoe in an orchard of smashed apricot, I hold it
        to my ear like cinders of snail shell, I hear persistence & meadow
        grass gossip across past occurrences of super blue blood moons.)

Our reciprocal reaching, like poetry, is dactylic.
Volitant pigeons of your lips, thin,

palpitate vocal frequencies
beyond this two-dimensional surface like hyacinths,
grape hyacinths of rain.

The Shoemaker's Daughter

When December's waxing crescent moon resembles a white pepper,
NAGYMAMA gets vacuumed back into occupied Hungary.
Sedative-Hypnotics gallop heavy-boned down her lithified throat,
bat-swatting her echolocative uvula with their rhythm-blue tails.
Rice pudding icefall follows by quivering silver spoonful.
OPEN THE SLATTED GATE!
My dream ripens like an angel-
trumpet into a prehistoric forest where her ubiquitous
nocturnal pings are lightning splitting deciduous beech.
Where tyrannies' stereoscopic scent hound snouts
desecrate wetlands, wheat fields, proboscises
sucking bone marrow from earth-built homes, ectoparasitic.
Kleptoparasitic—swarming willowing villages.
Sugar, bowls, jam, pots, sauce, pans, stale bread, spoiled
meat, precious lives now belonged
to dictators, politicians, occupying soldiers. What not-yet-radio-
active May-bells will hypersonically unscroll pitch-redolent like elastic accordion
bellows, petrichored, out from alkaline dirt? What windblown warning note
I once composed for her post-
broken-porcelain will glitter my inscriptions? Fluvial signals
from a future in which she cannot firefly jar
my name. She cannot lift
my botanical harbinger toward her face. She zeroes in on a distant
iridescent pigeon. Her private focal point for survival. My failed holographic mail.
(May you soon sniff dew music on winter—
its sickle moon's saline hair.)
SHUT THE SLATTED GATE!
In her bronchial orchards blushing ochre, apricots
descend like tank explosives, ferment
along that corridored kaptárkő of her thoracic cage. Rot-
bewitched wasps rattle, pneumonic. She vomits
a stiff pigeon foot gripping a pinwheel bouquet of bile-wrinkled letters.
In our true future, I stick my hand through her arboreal urn

to place dragon meat beneath her withered tongue unlike a prescription drug.
OPEN THE KNITTED GATE!
The cellar shelter displacing time like a water bug. Did she hide
behind potato-congested buckets? (When I visit her village there is a depression
left the shapesize of a woman's seismographic body.) After planting
pork meat bulbs in floorboard soil, after lakefoam mold growth, after brewing
incendiary weapons like potions, exodus bloomed, pathogenic.
SHUT THE KNITTED GATE!
Today, I bring her red wine for its antimicrobial properties.
Today, I bring her VALCSI NÉNI's Zserbó cake baked with flour of feledékenység.

Dysautonomia

C3

You shouldered your Prunus village here post-revolution,
buried verdant & rattling in your neverending purse
from which I picked poppy ash & pogácsa
crumbs like snow crystals, precious stones, dew-vitreous
frozen foliage, eusocial insects, mother-of-pearl
synonyms. From which I pulled
a wine-dark garland of parched red peppers like an ancestral amuletic necklace.
In THE KILMER REFUGEE CAMP did your purse burp up indigestible
apricot pits moon-dimpled with homesickness? Could you even carry
a purse in plum-nights of November sneaking through
a militarized barbed wire curtain? Beyond a minefield?

C6

You shouldered your Prunus village here post-revolution. I dove
ritualistically into inverted radicled earth of your neverending purse,
my palms together, a telluric prayer parting
detrital surfaces—hilly riverine torso, half-myth, holographic
transient dream. At the entrance, inexorable
apricot orchard, hypnogelic. By cawing drupes by crowing blossoms
I was welcomed in a familiar dialect of burnt-yellow, my neural tissue bridge-lit.

T4

Enwreathed by Bükk & Zemplén mountains,
Pauline Monastery ruins, I placed
dried lotus pod wreaths graveside in our Northeastern howling garden.
I brushed soil away from DÉDANYA's blackberry-cane meadow grave with sheaves of wheat,
I brushed soil away from DÉDAPA's banished mountainside grave with sheaves of wheat.
To the time signature of my four-chambered barometer, I spelled a word
I could not have possibly known with the phantom branches of my body;

I soil-angeled amidst a terroir of river mist & andesitic rhyolitic tuff,
translated silver rain clouds into mute swan song. If only I had
baked mythical biscuits with nyirok or yellow earth or rock flour.
If only I had distrusted time.

T8

Whenever I opened my blood-sucking beak,
you regurgitated homesick pigeon
milk like a tonic. Whenever your body violined dissonance for your mother,
I spoon-fed you volcanic sediment like sugar.
Whenever you swineherd-horned your longing through linden,
the Hungarian Grey herd in your neverending purse panicked
toward the Hungarian Grey herd in the pasture of my abdomen.
The wind plectrumming their lyre-like horns.
(A post-volcanic confluence of keratin.)

T12

My whole girlhood long I longed & longed for volcanic loam,
for the fungal bones of my forrobinieaemothers.
Their true ribs—splintering wooden spoons!
Their pelvic girdles—scorching copper cauldrons!
O stone ruins cob-webbing my sternum,
O sacral orchards erupting pedunculate oak,
O fossa echoic with ubiquitous dog song,
is dysautonomia post-death happenstance, comorbidity, viral aftermath, devotion?
How can I trust my body if I could not trust hers?

L2

I descended into DÉDANYA's dark pince—
domestic viscera—from which my mother afraid once
retrieved potatoes hibernating in
potato-congested buckets, behind which her mother
may or may not have hid afraid during occupation.

Above—

A wasp waded in the ocherous wetlands of sárgabarack jam.
A sunflower faced the sun devotedly for hours.

Above—

A child lost in a piac, my mother is unrelentingly without her mother.
The sunflower's face becomes a pollinated instruments' sound chamber.

(Transoceanic)

L4

I filamented myself inside out our Prunus post-volcanic village;
our Northeastern howling garden resembling an impacted dental radiograph. My unknown mouth
wild-dry, salivary glands susurrating with antibodies, I heat-sought
the molars of my forrobinieaemothers' graves without names. My fingertips like isotach roosters,
I hunted wind-thrumming enameled gravestones, which dispersed upon contact into
a mischief of locomotive tickets. Sweet tooth after sweet tooth,
my own mouth palate-staticked with ice particles, with fractoemissions.

S1

In the Prunus village you shouldered here post-revolution,
ICA NÉNI fermented
sárgabarack in blue plastic barrels like a network of volcanic conduits.
I ingested her barackpálinka brew—
Do I remember being welcomed home by you, inflamed with the dust of paprika?
Do I remember remembering being welcomed home by you insulated in pyroclastic spice?
Do I remember my mother reminding me you welcomed me home in your édesnemes speech?
Do I remember remembering my mother reminding me you welcomed me erubescently home?
NAGYMAMA—what exactly are the vertebral tectonics of memory, slipping?
My autonomic nervous system is (like the butterfly of your lungs) failing.
How can I depend upon my body if I could not depend upon yours?

THE SHAPE OF MY BODY IS DUST

: in taciturn domiciliary angles

water never reaches The hands
rain-wrinkled
like blood I want a departure
resolving in return
desperate for a rhythm hurried
dirt-hymns arrows pressing ribs
milk-blue-marsh thistles
if my body is her body
the wind means
she might be
everywhere

: in her gossamer sweaters

which gather failed rememberings
implacable fabric lakes
dispersing gravitational remains of
femur-thick murmurs
words rivered from her mouth
I preserve them here
where skin encounters skin
I can believe in something
rummaging
in such subtle places
because hackled guard-haired angels are
wingéd self-decorating keys

: in lilahagyma skins unswept

still fragrant
I fold myself inward A little beaked letter
uterine dusk
mouthfuls of chamomile chrysanthemums
veining the sky inverted map
in a moment sustained like a scar
I join you
in devotion
in the volcanic clay of a faraway village
erupting
lichened gravestones resembling
misplaced
milk-rotten deciduous teeth.

Snowfield

1

Purple gnarled knots deoxygenated blood oxygenated blood

IMPOSSIBLE MAP

oxygenated blood deoxygenated blood purple gnarled knots

snowfield. Where do you go vanishing—NAGYMAMA?   —Thou canst hear though from the wild—
A descaled butterfly wing (A skeleton flower).

I skein myself rapacious tracing your musicbox migrations.

2

You have no teeth left. Grief
logic states: spell your name with baby teeth.
You have no keys left. Grief
logic states: spell your name with skeleton keys.

Your name—ARANKA—
Transylvanian gate I remain beneath.

Above me,

iridescent pigeons exit your gate's trigonal pigeonholes full of
ink & funerary urns & wind eggs & never return

inside:

A   VOLCANICLASTIC LAKE FORMED IN AN ABANDONED MILLSTONE QUARRY

(R)

A   SESSILE OAK FOREST FROM WHICH BOTRYTIZED WINE CASKS ARE MADE

(NK)

A   CARPATHIAN VILLAGE ORCHESTRATING ANNUAL APRICOT FIESTAS

No keys to you I hold your hand like a doorknob.

You momentarily open:

Why is losing you synonymous with losing me?   —Mother hear a suppliant child!—
A ~~Because I am your country~~ A What is this word SYNONYMOUS?

You wave the word away like a szúnyog with your whisk broom hand.
The word decomposes like flesh. Its two umbilical Os glow beneath

our loveseat like live coals.   —The flinty couch we now must share—
      —Shall seem with down of eider piled—

: Your quivering mouth

A pressing wind Wh—   Am I? (Skeleton flower, repel the rain.)

Your táragató throat blows corroded words that float like sour cherries
in the cold-summer-soup bowls of my eardrums. Mit árul el a por?

3

Sundowning is—

your eyes rabid & quicksilver-sharpened by

the blistering panic of NOWHERENESS NOT AT ALL
originating from the spiral web of EVERYWHERENESS ALL AT ONCE.

Your past of horsehair scratching
against your present of ruminant intestines

(O friction) I witness your body violining for something
familiar. Grief logic states: reupholster. Stitch

your twisted knobbly memory-fabric
to oaken furniture (A figment A projection)

transforming into your mother
ANNA four-legged, carnivorous, resurrected.

Is a chair inorganic, organic?
She lets loose a lunar marcescent creak

—synonymous with Lycanthropy

4

Dementia folds the beautiful chair
you would have become

the needlework of
if only the memory reverie had lasted long enough.

5

The music therapist says: O you have such a pretty gate!
The music therapist defibrillates you with Ave Maria,

flips up your spine's T2 light switch with a guitar pick.

Then, your half-smile. The brief beacon I live for.   —Shall breathe of balm if thou hast smiled—

Does your deceased-by-suicide graveyard-banished father DEZSŐ

with his Pernambuco & whalebone bow
play back catgut-slashed songs? Hello

for the hundredth time today
you rise suspicious in the baby monitor in the hospital bed

inflating deflating you hallucinate—
bake walnut cake with your loose doorknobs

& invisible ingredients

FORGETFUL FLOUR SILENCED SUGAR EXODUSED EGGS

place the oxygen tube
in your mouth—finally found your missing set of teeth!

Every day I knead you every day I lose you
NOWHERENESS NOWHERENESS   —From this their wonted haunt exiled—

Snowfield.

Howler Tone

A Where am I? M Index finger like a corn-broom brushing
corridored surface corridored surface. What does dust disclose?

A Who are you for me? M Vampire finch beak encouraging blood,
I am your daughter's daughter, do you remember? Her Racka horn ear

Trumpet (This is HUNGER   HUNGAR-)
H   A ladder with one lachrymal rung necessary to replace a charred sun before nightfall.

        I climb the backs of your mother's gyönyörű székek beautiful chairs! To get to—

A Which country? M Your girlhood village descaled;
dwellings deroofed, pastures degrassed, skeletal sárgabarackfák.

—A yellow templeom undulating; A buoy in a graveyard rainstorm
—Au- tumnal templeom dropping vault angels like brittle leaves

—A theater whose seats shed red antler velvet
—Au- reate theater whose seats rot like milk teeth

. . . .

You suck bone marrow from fiddle spines

I am your daughter's daughter Do you remember? Her

. . . .

You pick mák from false teeth with lyre spines

I am your daughter's Do you remember?

. . . .

You replace your spine regularly with shield spines

I am Do you remember?

. . . .

Ameloglyphics

EIGHT PATTERNS OF ENAMEL ROD ENDS

~~WAVY BRANCHED~~

A   A CHE

~~STRAIGHT~~

R IGHT

~~LINEAR~~

EAR

~~TURNING LOOPS~~

R ING   OO

~~WAVY~~ UN~~BRANCHED~~

A   UN A CHE

~~O~~PEN WHO~~RLS~~

PEN WHO

~~BRANCH~~ING

R   ING

~~LOOP~~

OO

R~~ADIAT~~ING

R   ING

35

Estefelé / Toward Evening

you un-become in becoming autumnal. You relinquish aromatic remembrance
after aromatic remembrance. You relinquish onion, marjoram, mulberry wine.
You relinquish caraway, cauldron of copper or clay, name after name
Even The Anna Grove Old Oak of Szarvas,   even mine.

O tousled meanwhile of anonymity in which you glisten like a candle-kissed bloodhound—
Here are my syllabic handkerchiefs gold-blossoming almost apparitional
scents of citrus. Relocate our relation for I am bereft of you. Won't you unscatter
your narrative from untraceable directions & harmonica yourself back?

Emlékek / Remembrances

tearing wind like undisciplined silverware of fingers. Be gravitational
with the sacred magnitude of a kitchen. I did not dare ask: what if
amidst winter solstice occurs a solar eclipse & you are gone? What then?
I did not dare ask: where am I to find a furnace? (Ours once stoked itself.)

O vertebral hearth broom O pulmonic bellow This exact taxonomy of devotion is—

csontképződés / ossification.

How our bones (rusted peafowl-blue) train-rattle arthritic like branches
familiar with exquisite abscission. What's left of you NAGYMAMA
if not a bosom of sugar with which to dust the crescent-shaped
sweet bread of inherited grief-porcelain? What's left of
NAGYPAPA's lánytestvérek if not inflammation,

darázsfészek / a nest of wasps,

neuropathic extremity after neuropathic extremity? My skin is wreath-making.
I suffer vulturous globe thistles. Amethyst-skulled. Hook-leafed.
I suffer a thousand celestial arrows. Lost in that labyrinthine
meanwhile you spell-casted. And you are no longer here
peace-offering pain: eperdzsem cédrusfa százszorszép pitypang.

Phytoremediation (Ars Therapoetica)

Sunflower vascular systems buried-suture
the hem of DÉDANYA ANNA's Northeastern howling garden with
the etymological root of NAGYMAMA's name—
ARANY ARANY ARANY
O sunflower with your sugar equation,
may I become your humble
apprentice in synthesizing breath & water for growing
by an orchestra of light. Teach me your self-tending alchemy.
Or am I singing now of half-illusions?
O sunflower extracting radioactive contaminants from soil,
how I have rotated my own pseudanthium in solar devotion,
how I have rusted my stalk stuck & leaning
in NAGYMAMA's directionless direction. I—
like you—phytoremediate. A recursive platter stomach
the substance of responsibility, resentment, recalcitrance, reluctance.
A porous identified-patient vessel.
A heliotropic sieve. Here I rely on narrative pollination,
extracting silences, nightmares, tough-to-slough-off behaviors like heavy metals from ŐSAKÁCFÁIM.
(Where has NAGYMAMA's oral historic hummingbird gone,
migrating backwards upside down?
And her powdery yellow correspondences?)
True: a poem—like a pondful of genealogical wine—is a ritual of reaching.
Here I rely on tavern-dancing bulls volant
& blood-letting therapeutically like volcanoes
into hollow cumulonimbus sinuses resembling dragonflies.
Here KÉKFRANKOS-congested thunderclouds blow their bloody noses
& I get drenched in NAGYMAMA's loessed befores.
O dried lotus pod wreaths graveside do tell me:
what nonviable coordinate pair is this now?
Our timelines—are they chimneyed trains
that will never again brush glass panes?
My ears are cricketing with the nolongerness of you.
I would beg these village dogs rescind their dirt-hymns,

I would beg the yellow templom like a lighthouse still its omnidirectional bell,
but O how I would then thin & thin
the buckled mouths of earth-built roofless houses depending upon
daily echoic breakfasts. (A village rejoicing in apricot jam!)
O how I would then unthread the sonic threads
once scoring your Prunus village girlhood
that have up until now braided
my spinal ligaments structurally sound, unsound.

48.47099°N 21.27417°E

i

Decaying cuspid gates growing

out from rain-

swollen gingival ground

(like carrots

upturned)

Violet car-

rots The inviolate Once

of red tiles worshipped

by solstitial sun

Touched A

memory remains

untouched

Stone house without   A

roof Hear me

she is gone now (& I will not

have wept her back

tendon to tendon

marrow to marrow

ii

Ő nádtető

O sheaves of wheat O wetland reeds

Stone house without   A

roof you are—

        weed-veined (wild garlic)

        water-scarred (sacred ink)

        brick-wombed (history is kicking)

iii

NAGYMAMA

I am sorry I broke (again)

into your Reliquary of Remembrances

But my hands

they are becoming

your hands

The last word

I learned from you—

      gyulladás

iv

And when my hands

are finally (inflamed)

your hands

together we will brush

the deciduous hair—

together we will flask

the lachrymal narrative—

of Szomorúfűzfá

MOLTING IN THE MÁTRA MOUNTAINS

DEAR VOLCANO, WHERE ARE YOU?
—Traci Brimhall, "Dear Thanatos,"

When I prepared, especially, a porcelain vessel of wild
sour cherries for your transparent palms, atmospheric, let loose
to pierce each cinder-block surface like paws of village dogs. Since you respond
neither in analytic nor agglutinative language, I hemorrhage
finch song like silvering gibberish. It was all before. Before
a subliminal hunger for rhyolitic andesitic earthworms,
before slime-insulated successions of amnestic Decembers.
Before such redundance of dawns erupting incessant
rain-hot embers glowing memory-delicate. The inevitable
wing violin-bowing my larynx, June-spilling
Tisza blooms. Before unspooling away from space-
tetherless nights. Dear air-
plane, when did you digest yourself into a rift
lake, then imaginal disc yourself into a nesting doll varnished
in her traditional embroidered garments? Eclose, finally, from your exoskeleton
a duet of asymmetric lungs? In my melting dreams, I resurrect her
so that I may dress her in silk night-
gowns stitched with tuliped fabric of palliative words.
It is much too intergalactic, our never-happened goodbye.
An earth-measurer moth, I have lost myself
to the lantern of your ONCE. The moon of my future,
my point of reference, my positive phototaxis,
my navigational system, my nocturnal intelligence,
all bewildered, all disrupted by the hypnotist of
matriviticultural psychic inheritance swinging her pocket
watch here, there. Before I witnessed
my hands become plum, my grandmother's hands become snow,
it was before I accordioned my body into her arboreal urn,
eating off my very own ankles, wrists, limbs, sifting ossein. A type of love bubbling
tongue-scarring hot like puszta stew rich with paprika & stories.

I ladle myself into her ash-jar the size of an event horizon.
It was a time when my grandmother spoke
an indehiscent language a language of horses. Dear ruins, fill my ears with
Prunus brandy if you desire even a blink of knowing devotion
in spite of the presence of venom. I knocked
on your death's Danubian door
& you spooned sturgeon roe upon my tongue—
a black-gold alphabet. It was all before spondaic
passerine song, before twin belfries within
which your Balaton blue iris blue iris got
hammered by history. I shepherded myself forward
amidst a reverie wherein forward
means all other possible if impractical directions.
Must know the scent of your dormant dentures by now.
Must know the weight of your fake pearl earrings
as if pupae. Put your transparent palms
through my diaphragm. Tell me again: UNTIL YOU ARE YOUNG.
Dear metronome, weathervane, pendulum.
Dear sundial, my name is shadowless & I am unknown because of it too.
Rhythmically, I brush against every surface she once touched, leaving behind
an aftermath of seasonal diaphanous houses.

Sugar Geometry

opale-

scent (O her lard-stained apron unspooling

music of scaled tooth after scaled tooth;

a Balatonian school of tuning   forks!)

In NAGYMAMA's kávé   ring of melting pearls like a moon-

dial My small girl self again

in our former kitchen where withered umbilical cords

web beneath the floor

NAGYMAMA's teaspoon   silver uvula spelling O

skimming her teacup's scalloped mouth

(O—A gate I key with

the dragonflied tongue of my unfamiliar name)

Resonance

Epiphanic

Five days after we swept up dust & ate poultry instead of lentils

She died dawn of Vízkereszt

Apricot stones pinioned & lilting in

a Herend bowl nest

Lint beginnings (I still fit

in the sweaters she once knit for me)

Pedunculate oak & orange orchard be-

longings I was not there

but the peripheral nerve endings of skin—

where the lost limb that is her youth

had once been—

send pain signals like beaks

my brain receives I remember

ripe red ornaments (NAGYMAMA would gum like pacifiers

in phantom-briared dreams)

Lard in a jar by the stove On bread

Haunted bread

Boiled cabbage leaves Her bed linens

Translu-

cent Why did we clean them?

A Pogácsa Pantoum For Posthumous Love

I am sifting the all-purpose flour of language
for that which is synonymous with BODILESSNESS.
A dictionary is laminated dough sowed with scratchings
& baked in the spine-binding ash of matriviticultural wisdom.
Distance depends upon whether
I let my perspective be limited by fact of flesh.
If flame-blue vague, a polyphonic howl of vapor, split-second-peripheral.
If ENTANGLEMENT, I forbid limits on the miracles of love.

My risen dictionary is laminated dough baked in the spine
binding ash of matriviticultural wisdom, into which I scratch telluric prayers.
Preserving rhythm with my own neuropathic hands, you integrate milk & yeast for mother
tongue brushed mythical biscuits. If winter oven heat,
if hummingbird, if single split strand of saved hair or orb-weaver spider Y-spelling synchronously
in horizontal & vertical planes. I forbid limits on the mysteries of love.
I become briefly reticent reflective before grated white-green cabbage
resembling the drenched diaphanous fractal grass
that steamed beneath the clay-caked soles of my feet
during your crescentless vigil. Shadow

playing with my own neuropathic hands,
you integrate yolk & sour cream,
butter & dragon meat for womb-baked mythical biscuits.
By freshwater kitchen sink rift lakes whose scaled silverware lungs are
inflamed neither by pneumonia nor sludge,
I ungently ingest grated white-green cabbage
resembling the drenched diaphanous fractal grass
that steamed beneath the clay-caked soles of my feet
during your wolf-enwreathed vigil.
If atmospheric. If embryonic. If omniscient
red stag. If RESPLENDENT SILHOUETTE.

Oak-table-shading nearby freshwater kitchen sink rift lakes
whose Poales plastic lungs are inflamed
neither by pneumonia nor sludge,
I internalize 1 river resistance
2 grapevine veins pollinated by wind
3 an amniotic pond winter-stiffened.
If trace fossil time-kept or pollen vectored. If locomotive-pane-brushing
red stag. If RAGYOGÓ SZILUETT.
If you are proximate & ubiquitous
please answer this: why is my body attacking itself?

Will internalizing 1 river-resistance
2 grapevine veins pollinated by wind
3 an amniotic pond winter-stiffened heal me?
A warning is bear garlic folded into dictionary dough;
emerald stain after emerald stain signaturing pages!
If you are proximate & ubiquitous
help me understand why my body is attacking itself.
Dear Physician: here is the indecipherable
alphabet of my plasma
(O blood-whisperings elusive & pleated.)

A promise is bear garlic folded into dictionary dough;
emerald stain after emerald stain signaturing pages!
Q: What are the linguistic properties of posthumous love?
A: The roots, tuning
forks, antennae, wings, knitting
pins, bird binoculars, horseshoe magnets, barking
binary star system of diacritics stretching beyond death's distances.
Dear Physician: here is the indecipherable
alphabet of my plasma
(O blood-whisperings oblique & devious.)
Q: What are the medicinal properties of posthumous love?
A: Acacia's viscous fingers born from insect digestion,
a chiliad kiss, kamilla's wild-mother-blue fingers rewriting crossed wiring.

The medicinal properties of posthumous love—
blue-mother-wild, chiliad kissed.
An epilogue depends upon whether
I let my perspective be limited by fact of flesh.
Are you listening—?
The bolts of my blood are ephemeral yet pearlescent.
O BODILESSNESS O ENTANGLEMENT
O RESPLENDENT SILHOUETTE,
I forbid limits on the magic of love.

Death Rattle Aubade

Terminal respiratory secretions or   hoof-time   of vanishment?

A baby rattle   within her pharynx   resembling a mirrored honey dipper   see-sawing

Visceral beans knocking prescience or   herd of ancient Podolic cattle   silver & stampeding in-verse?

Riverine throat   She is guided now by her own salival rhythm   Oar-chestrating a coda

What is the etymology of a river?   Dew-drop born   She is gondola-shaped in death

A percussive snake   Her lopsided spine buoyant & blooming

From placental Black Forest (O glucose of oak)   To Black Sea galloping toward

aftermath   I hear her

O lyre-like horns

What is the osteometric record of migratory music?

I craft a harmonica from pneumatic swan skeletons

Stethoscopic I listen for syllabic palpitations   I see you I saw you

What goes up in sound must come down in silence

She who was with us in dusk is by dawn no longer

Death's corridor is a corn poppy meadow where a chord of Danubian meadow vipers becomes—

A triangular welcome rug   An ancestral tambourine   An unspooling mother tongue

Dress Resurrection

The scrolled spears of ICA NÉNI's iron gate
accordioned like sweet-dream-
black ribs with wind's respiratory rhythms.
From her palpitating house—
veined with wheat-gold grape vines
arteried with internodal rhizomes
capillaried with eusocial honey storms
—ICA NÉNI's gaze radiated you SEE THROUGH.
EMLÉKSZEM. An open sesame.
Your temporal lobe stretched,
sunbathing, oiling its plumage.
A pike perch skeleton haunting poisoned rivers,
punishing billionaires with temporary gills,
swished its hour hand tail
& you—MY NINE-YEAR-OLD MOTHER—got revived by
an oak-smoked gallop of bogrács broth.
If industrial sludge staining rivers
with cyanide & caustic waste had not killed thousands of
tons of folyó fish across seasons,
the pikeperch alive & hissing about
noctalgia in meteorological dialects of
obscuration & precipitation would have sprouted
twelve heads & two iridescently scaled wings after seven years.
ICA NÉNI wood-winded blood like jelly *fresh*
into familiar cadaverous fabric of a misplaced memory:
the dress you once mended together with thread like breath
along a leafy corridor bursting ribizli bokrok
amidst a grove hiccupping miraculous sárgabarackfák.
The resurrected dress resembling a diaphragm
or a kite embroidered uterine red
& gestational scar white (O picnic phantom!)
shape-shifted into the plumaged cradle
that first lullabied you home post-revolution,

melted into the polymictic shadow of the plumaged cradle
sunflower field skating on rosined fiddle wheels.
The resurrected dress tip-toed behind you as if
your almost-brother's placental parachute,
slumped eventually upon your soundholed back;
the calcinated acres of NAGYMAMA's death, post-disbelief.

Matriviticultural Transfusions

After toasting NAGYMAMA's posthumous health
raising my scooped palms, their pondfuls of KADARKA blend,
a wingéd bull tavern-dances me backforth in imperfect time—

To EGRI MAMA ladling savory gulyás lakes
into vast clay bowls (O potato & parsnip boats!)
To her red straw-braided basket bassineting bread;

a blood moon, a broken minute
hand making multidirectional revolutions
around checkered tablecloth.

Where NAGYMAMA is the diaphragmatic violin ribboning
amidst that mapless out-of-reach distance,
& scrolls of forrobinieaemotherly initial-arborglyphs

ravel unravel like fern fronds, like beckoning fingers,
out from a silver harmonica, out from a shepherd's flute.
Where my neuropathic legs are entangled with primeval beech roots!

Where white violets drape acrobatically bat-like from baskets
& endangered Clouded Apollos pollinate my allopecian hair.
A wingéd bull tavern-dances me backforth in imperfect time—

To grapevines tended by women whose haunting I no longer eat like buttercream
sponge cakes made of drums, like bacon lard biscuits baked in ash;
filled with goldsilver forint coins, filled with pigeon feathers.

To grapevines tambourining with cricket script!
At dusk I listen with my POTS blood
volume, kúszónövény leveleket.

Transfusing sacred choral knowledge into my dysfunctional circulatory system,
transfusing cyclic moon knowledge into my tendrilled & leafy root vessels.

Gooseflesh

a konyhában   anyád konyhája   a konyhaasztal alatt . . .
a konyhában   anyád konyhája,   a konyhaasztal alatt . . .
in the kitchen   your mother's kitchen   under the kitchen table . . .
in the kitchen   your mother's kitchen   under the kitchen table . . .

a konyhában   anyád konyhája   a konyhaasztal alatt . . .
a konyhában   anyád konyhája   a konyhaasztal alatt . . .
in the kitchen   your mother's kitchen   under the kitchen table . . .
in the kitchen   your mother's kitchen   under the kitchen table . . .

1

NAGYMAMA's handmade
embroidered tablecloth enshrouding

you MOTHER folding yourself—a letter

Is your hand unexpectedly warm now? Itching suddenly of
loose onion skins like crow feathers? Unswept dust & crumbs? I am

there. There,
my hand enveloping yours (a sponge

from which I wring sludgy river water
your girlhood ceiling weeps)

I comb the kamilla of my palm over the scroll of your forearm
ciphering A GOOSEFLESH ALPHABET

2

Two of two hundred thousand Magyars gone
in s / ear / ch of refuge

A cauldron counterclockwise NAGYMAMA's kitchen table

Her hour hand—a decanter of barackpálinka
the decanter drops

s p   l

O cipher O stuck note   n   e
The organs sounds   s
                              i   t
& sounds   r

3

A pressing wind

Wh—   Am I?

Your Racka horn ear trumpet: (To better hear!)

A spiral-shaped umbilical cord pulsing
A spiral-shaped phantom limb burning   *ibolyák tulipánok paprikás szőlő indák madarak , . .*
                                           violets tulips paprika grapes tendrils birds . . .
                                                      ibolyák tulipánok paprikás szőlő indák madarak . .
                                                      violets tulips paprika grapes tendrils birds . . .
Magyars' placental mouths provide   *ibolyák tulipánok paprikás szőlő indák madarak . . .*
clockwise NAGYMAMA's kitchen table   *ibolyák tulipánok paprikás szőlő indák madarak , . .*
                                           violets tulips paprika grapes tendrils birds . . .

You receive nutrient-rich earfuls facefuls but you grow thin
If plasmatic narrative clogs your pores, apply your sunflower oil egg yolk sugar

& black locust honey mask!

A knitted gate of displaced legs encloses you
The polyphony oxygenates & overshadows you

O mother-tongued pigeons   sticky with exodic yolk

. . . .

Let me hear too!   Let me here too!
                     Let me here too!
                     Let me here too!

. . . .

I listen I grip my millstone tooth (my ticket!)   I wolf down mák soil ash

Iridescent pigeons nest like nonsensical sentences in my unbrushed bat roost hair
I swallow amniotic liquor distilled from foaming apricots

The organ sounds

"... *Every Hungarian living far*
from his country unless he has definitely lost

his human character is waiting
for the day when he will be able to go home ..."

"... *Every Hungarian living far*
from his country unless he has definitely lost
"... *Every Hungarian living far*
from his country unless he has definitely lost
his human character is waiting
for the day when he will be able to go home ..."
his human character is waiting
for the day when he will be able to go home ..."

4

What were your own main reasons for living far?
I almost ask the cauldron at the table by way of gooseflesh.

ƒ   [hole]   ear   ƒ   [hole]   ear

Her hour hand A decanter of barackpálinka
The decanter rises Re-

comb

     i

          e

               n

                    s

ibolyák tulipánok paprikás szőlő indák madarak ...
violets tulips paprika grapes tendrils birds ...
ibolyák tulipánok paprikás szőlő indák madarak ...
violets tulips paprika grapes tendrils birds ...

Presently NAGYMAMA's urna feathering
To release the sixteen rock doves of her body

when they will be able to go home
when they will be able to go home
when they will be able to go home
when they will be able to go home
when they will be able to go home

Presently NAGYPAPA's urna feathering
To release the thirty-two rock doves of his

                         far
from   lost

            waiting

5

A KONYHÁBAN A KONYHÁMBAN A KONYHAASZTAL ALATT VAGYOK
In the kitchen in my kitchen I am under the kitchen table

anticipating a graphesthesiac letter
swallowing barackpálinka

mothering my mother who mothered her mother
who mothered her mother

Reliving NAGYMAMA's death in exquisite detail
(O how women surround women)

embroidering this page like she embroidered this tablecloth.

ibolyák tulipánok paprikás szőlő indák madarak
violets tulips paprika grapes tendrils birds

ibolyák tulipánok paprikás szőlő indák madarak
violets tulips paprika grapes tendrils birds
ibolyák tulipánok paprikás szőlő indák madarak
violets tulips paprika grapes tendrils birds
violets tulips paprika grapes tendrils birds

Piroska (Little Red Riding Hood)

ACROSS SEVEN COUNTRIES THROUGH THE SEA OF ÓPERENCIA THROUGH THE GLASS MOUN-TAINS ONCE UPON A TIME WHERE SHE ONCE WAS WHERE SHE ONCE WAS NOT—The propulsive force with which I go backforth toward a volatile elusive phantasmic ONCE is nothing like an arrow fixed on a singular focal point but rather like a weather vane whose beak's direction is determined entirely by prefer-ences, gradations, intuitions of wind. When I write A time, I mean A-time: my NAGYMAMA A's time. But also prefix denoting not or without. Thus, Once upon A time that is not time or is without time or unsettles perceptions of time because very much unlike you (LÁNY AKI VOLTAM VALAHA) I do grasp object perma-nence of bellowing befores. When their past hides from you it no longer exists. When their past hides from me I wait—A woman within a woman within a woman.

They existed like a matrilineal Matryoshka doll painted in embroidered folk-clothes, frequently reshuffling themselves into reverse agesize order, each descendant breaking its own flexible bones, inflating itself like a balloon, incapsulating the onion-mother that sprung before whenever post-memorially necessary. Two years after The Revolution—When I write Revolution I mean October–November student-worker uprising against Soviet occupation for democratic reforms but I also mean ever-rotation. For NAGYMAMA The Revolution was not a single past event. It is an unspooling. An enwreathing. An exodus eating itself—1958 A doubled with her first pregnancy; her first (but not only) daughter, who would one day lose the knowledge of exactly how long A (whose name means gold) was held in Camp Kilmer with her husband L (who ostensibly escaped starved from a forced labor camp where a soldier whipped the soles of his feet into ribbons & knocked out his back teeth like rocks). While buoyant in A's uterus A's first daughter E basketed in her small body of linden all the eggs she would ever divine like dough. Meaning E's first & only daughter was there too. In late 1958 early 1959 every song A had sung The Egg had heard too. The Egg had sensed every warm & pulsing handprint on A's skin, A's psychoemotional fluctuations became E's psychoemotional fluctuations became The Egg's psychoemotional fluctuations. A's organs churned & wrung from military force. When A (ENGLISHLESS) spoke Hungarian in New Jersey her organs churned & wrung with vowel harmony. When A's own mother died in A's occupied motherland, A developed a depthless appetite for volcanic detritus. A's pained organs became E's panged organs became The Egg.

E grew in a painful uterus. E gnawed on Magyar like a pacifier before any other language. The Egg warped into an ear rusted stuck in the direction of Magyar. When A had gulyás, hortobágyi palacsinta, sour cherry soup, E viscerally danced The Csárdás in imperfect time & The Egg bounced up & down. When A had sweet poppy seed noodles, beigli, strudel, E viscerally danced The Csárdás in imperfect time & The Egg bounced up & down. A hummed & heated mangalica lard on medium-high. A's apron yellowed with Lassan-Friska tempo-change-stains, reddened with eruptions of paprika.

Imperfect time—

Whole note

        M   o   ther 1 systole 2 diastole

        F   o   etus 3 systole 4 diastole

Decades later E gave birth.

P (AKA The Egg)—In Magyar tradition pre-Christianity eggs were dyed red (meaning renewal) with lilahagyma skins. Messages were scratched upon eggs. Half-circles representing resurrection—was born of tűz (etymologically speaking), figuratively but literally too, for E hemorrhaged during labor. In 1995 E nearly died. P was named Piroska deriving from a Latin name meaning ancient but directly meaning red after the Hungarian word piros. Some say when E gave birth, P (lustrous with blood) had red tulip petals red corn poppy petals resting froglike on her tongue, ribbiting prescience.

When P metamorphized into a woman herself, A began losing her memory. Her exteroceptive & interoceptive sensation-remembrances hid volatile elusive phantasmic but not like ONCE (The Very Thing Itself)—Remember time does not simply blow in one forward direction. Time blows backwards obliquely vertically vortexing. At the end of the world, The Wind Mother whips a whirlwind like a spinning top inside of the mirage of a melting navel-clock—A's exteroceptive & interoceptive sensation-remembrances hid instead like self-decorating insects; there but disguised (hypothermic purpling furniture, navel words bitter cruciferous verdant, locust leaflet refractions of heavy-metaled afternoon light, garbage truck dumpster detonations, air-raid siren mockingbirdsong & fire department noontimealarm, curdled cow milk in a carton labeled organic, hot vibrations of vanishing vocabularies furrowed eyebrow electricity, itchy whispers from a warren of sentient dust, unsolicited skin friction burning like a thicket). A lost P's name like a key, A lost E's name like a key, A lost her own name like a key. She weakened. She required sedative hypnotics, morphine, antipsychotics. After the sun went downing downing downing, A astral-projected; chrononautic. A philharmonicked with her dead. She died when they did (AKA wish-fulfillment). Reluctantly, she was revived!

One afternoon (1925 1956 2022) P brought A an elixir of Aszú wine—Aszú wine is a sweet dessert wine produced in Northeastern Hungary. It is the delicious result of a botrytized indigenous grape variety called FURMINT. The vital mold (Aszúsodás) raisoning FURMINT is called The Noble Rot. NAGYMAMA's birth county, Borsod-Abaúj-Zemplén, boasts rich volcanic clay & the ideal microclimate necessary for inducing The Noble Rot—& a walnut cake. A was only down the hall in her levitating bedroom. A was a forest away. A was a rift lake away. A was The Atlantic Ocean away. P walked through this gnarled knotted forest like a wall, over this vast field of red tulip & red corn poppy like a carpet. P crossed The Atlantic Ocean, got volcanic soil (rhyolite andesite obsidian) on the taste buds of her boots, on the hems of her locust-prickly trousers. She knocked like a woodpecker on the door. It was a minute later. It was hours later. Days. While walking through this gnarled knotted forest like a wall, over this vast field of red tulip & red corn poppy like a carpet, a presence followed P. The shadow had rotating wheels, true, but the soil betrayed paw prints. P knocked on the door. A was bed bound & feral. WORDLESS. P corresponded with A by inscribing air with hoofprints.

P corresponded, galloping fingers.

What big ears you have!
Milyen nagy füled van!

What big eyes you have!
Milyen nagy szemed van!

What big hands you have!
Milyen nagy kezed van!

What a horribly big mouth you have!
Milyen szörnyen nagy a szád!

A's ears big for listening forwards backwards obliquely vertically across vortexed calendars.
A's eyes big for visioning forwards backwards obliquely vertically across vortexed calendars.
A's hands big for reaching forwards backwards obliquely vertically across vortexed calendars.
A's mouth big for transmitting forwards backwards obliquely vertically across vortexed calendars.

THE BIGGER A FERAL REFUGEE GROWS IN STORYTELLING OF THE GYÜMÖLCSFÁK OF HOME,
THE SMALLER ÖRDÖGÖK OF POWER-MONEY-PROPAGANDA-GREED
WHO PLAY VICTIM, WHO WEAPONIZE AN IMPERIAL 'WOUND,' AND FOR WHOM
THE SKY KISSING TREES WILL NEVER BLOSSOM APPLES.

But when P approached A in her bed Her deathbed A was not A.

A was a Wolf A Hearse.

The Wolf The Hearse had swallowed A.

The Wolf then swallowed P—I recently had a dream that I was lying in NAGYMAMA's deathbed. I was in NAGYMAMA's body. NAGYMAMA was there in my body, at my bedside, holding my hand—whole (like a planet-eating parasite). Death began breathing fire & writing stories.

A huntswoman (they say) butterflied the wolf's stomach.

Though the Wolf swallowed both A & P & later E, the huntswoman found only one linden doll stacked shut like a moldy onion.

THE HEALER COUNTS BACKWARDS

INSTRUCTIONS: INCANT BY FILLING ALL BLANK SPACES WITH ONE HOMONYM
PER INCANTATION. CONSIDER THE TWO READINGS OF EACH HOMONYM. CONSIDER
HOW A VERB, LIKE A NOUN, IS AN ENTITY AND HOW A NOUN, LIKE A VERB, MOVES.
REPEAT WITH RELEVANT-TO-YOU HOMONYMS AS NECESSARY.

Ten maggots in my _____ one drops out nine left

    nine maggots in my _____ one drops out eight left

eight maggots in my _____ one drops out seven left

    seven maggots in my _____ one drops out six left

six maggots in my _____ one drops out five left

    five maggots in my _____ one drops out four left

four maggots in my _____ one drops out three left

    three maggots in my _____ one drops out two left

two maggots in my _____ one drops out one left

    one maggot in my _____ one drops out not a single scrap left.

HOMONYMS

VÁR	*castle*	*wait*
SZÍV	*heart*	*suck/draw*
SZÉL	*wind*	*edge*
SÍR	*grave*	*cry*
PARADICSOM	*tomato*	*paradise*
NŐ	*woman*	*grow*
LÉP	*spleen*	*honeycomb*
FOG	*tooth*	*hold*
ÉR	*brooklet*	*vein*
ÉG	*sky*	*burn*
DOB	*drum*	*toss*
		(to throw to the daughter)
		(to waft a kiss)

Horologium Oscillatorium

Winter will once again hollow
my sárgabaracklekvár jar
—formed from liquid sand—into
a shepherd's pipe, a spectral snailshell,
my somatic half of a string telephone
whose duplicate, like a tulip bulb inverted,
pings ultrasonic-discarnate in a house of ravens.
I blow a palmful of édesnemes paprikás
into my hollow sárgabaracklekvár jar
& Ilona (soil-swimming butterfly stroke)
receives epistolary powder pigeons by the holographic hundreds!
At witching hour
ANCESTRESSES translate my sárgabaracklekvár jar
into a bogrács cauldron with which I brew
my very own vulnerary version of gulyásleves.
Two tablespoons of moon-
lard heated on medium-high,
one tablespoon of wild acacia honey
whisked—like celestial milk—in.
Seven cloves of bioluminescence, minced.
Two pounds of stewing rock flour.
One teaspoon of freshly ground crystalline water ice
plus one teaspoon of freshly ground quartz
imported directly from The Bug Nebula
in constellation Scorpius.
In my reverie, I heal
my women forwards backwards
of tank craters & venom
like horologium oscillatorium.

Vertical Surfaces

Pressingly I scatter our kitchen with garlic exoskeletons.
Who am I if not NAGYMAMA's last disciple in
the dendrochronology of red onions? Matyryoshkaed remembrances—
ash-silver stampedes still billowing warmbloodedly in my stomach
as if anachronistic lava. I admit
I bear visceral knowledge of very little else save for the after-
math of shattered moonlets. I trust only
tree-time now. Dementia's domestic thicket was
a detrital lung we all lived
disoriented in like a cup
nest. NAGYMAMA turned & turned
increasingly nocturnal, grasping for bark-
varnished vertical surfaces. She scraped
serrated forewings together, resembling
a patrilineal violin formerly relinquished. She plucked
intestinal harp strings of time's
rotary telephone in desperation. Her dead
never responded, ultrasonic, ricocheting epistles
off our traditional horsehair water flasks. The hoof
of my faraway forrobinieaemother's equine familiar
transmutes itself into a glimmering raven the shapesize of
Helix Nebula. The shapesize of
BELATEDNESS. The midwinter-dark
bird then vaults such interrogative spears like cometary knots
from the transoceanic corridor of her trachea:
do you ululate this way—buckling stridulating
your abdominal temperature risen—for not having
tenderly combed your grandmother's moonlit mane
more often in flesh, for not having
warmed her hand more often in the celestial stew
ladle, medicinal wheel-barrow, twangling bearskin of yours
(prophetic)? LISTEN! I interject. The nymph I once was
in girlhood's softwood corrugated whoosh—

gripping NAGYMAMA's apron strings like space tethers—
is now a translucent shadow; an ex-
oskeleton knapsacking my anatomy of intrinsic luminosity.
This musical musculature is forrobinieaemother-given.
In a cicada chorus sick with shriveled hydrophobic wings I aria:
antibacterial barbs, defeat transgenerational grief's microbial organisms!
If only the residual oils of NAGYMAMA's fingerprints would
glow-in-the-dark like neon signs, like entrance & exit
runes. How every vertical inch of our kitchen like
a scratch & sniff sticker would retain her lactonic redolence.

1

THERE IS NO VOLCANICLASTIC LAKE FORMED IN AN ABANDONED MILLSTONE QUARRY

There is no bedroom brush-stroked
with the wet mucus trails of your yesterday motions.

(Weren't you leaving me
scent-signals? Salt? Antibacterial balms

for transgenerational circumpolar wounds?)

If your sugar cube locutions are still descending
from CUMULO-SUCROSE-SPEECH-CLOUDS,

still dispersing somewhere noncartographic in concentric circles,

then they are reverberating now upon
an inverted negative surface far far away,

for there is no volcaniclastic lake but the percussive muscle
memory of agglutinative language.

2

In that room where there is no room I light-paint insomniac unmaps
rippling with contour lines resembling arborescent rings.

I practice your arborglyphs,
dipping my horsehair brush in bioluminescent ink.

I practice your gastronomic measurements,
dipping my horsehair brush in mangalica lard,

inscribing walls with recipes for mythical ember-baked biscuits.

Here: I once measured your homesick mood—
elevations, depressions, zero relief.

Here: I once measured volumes of your voicefall.
The water in my right ear is a pigeon nest,

the water is cooing what is lost.

3

In that room where there is no room I record residual thermal energy—
the old volatile temperatures of

your emotional fluctuations. Dormant light fixtures,
hypothermic furniture, creaseless fabric, there is no such thing.

There is only the heat of ONCE.
What is the circumference of a sugar cube?

THERE IS NO SESSILE OAK FOREST FROM WHICH BOTRYTIZED WINE CASKS ARE MADE

The other you, stone you, silicified you tricking
an inverted negative gap, a tar-like body bag parting air

diagonal down implacable stairs,
horizontal beyond implausible doors.

Nothing beyond
our house was real (wasn't our forest

spelling your name?)

There is no forest but the contour lines of a PAST
psychogenic fugue state.

You left a trail of coordinates
behind like carawayed pogácsa crumbs.

You left a trail of hour hands
behind like carawayed pogácsa crumbs.

Nothing beyond our house was real.
They brought you beyond our house

into the stomach of a hearse,

a wolf.

THERE IS NO SESSILE OAK FOREST FROM WHICH BOTRYTIZED WINE CASKS ARE MADE

The window I watched you (other you stone you silicified you) depart from
the window I am standing before

am I standing here now?
The last place I saw you from:

its gravity.

How everything in my body became a moon.
My stomach my uterus my bones my nails my tongue became moons.

The wolf was gone. Under

the inverted negative surface (O far far away lake)
a pike perch swims in amnestic circles

while your lungs like crescented gondolas
like endangered butterfly wings buoy;

a familiar symmetry.

There is no sessile oak forest but the bronchial orchards
of inflamed lungs that failed us.

THERE IS NO CARPATHIAN VILLAGE ORCHESTRATING ANNUAL APRICOT FIESTAS

In that room where there is no room I lichen-paint insomniac unmaps
rippling with contour lines resembling Kékesztető climate data.

(Weren't you leaving me
sugar? Caraway for the indigestion of

your inescapable death? Zephyr
blue wings beckoning presciently?) I study

square inches of our interknitted fingerprints as if
spider silk or rings of swamp cypress trunks prehistoric & preserved

in sandstorm. There is no other way through this labyrinthine room.
There is no room but the wolf's stomach.

What is the circumference of bodilessness?

The wolf's stomach is a blood moon,
the blood moon is an entrance,

an entrance into the village where volcanic soil is veined with
the botanical in-utero memory of agglutinative language.

There is no village but time's bow broken,
tensionless. There is no time but clay.

Butcher Shop Rendezvous

As a rule, when the dead-living womenfolk of my family go hungry for absent fathers, together we take up residence in a butcher shop without geodetic coordinates. Our ecliptic stomachs groaning like ancestral locust, we bescroll inherited violins with carp spine bones saved after brewing fisherman's soup along riverbanks; their maple necks spewing musical staves! We tie up our bat roost hair with ruminant intestines, scarf down slow smoked salami stuffed with snow and ripened with NOBLE ROT mold. Blouse buttons leap away from our mangalica-lard-fried-bread fetuses kicking in our abdomens, bruising cartilage and ribs. Scarletting simultaneously with pleasure and self-disgust, we question why there is so much guiltshame for a girl in growing big, budding disruptive, and occupying space. We play HE LOVES ME / HE LOVES ME NOT with oxeye; a roulette of petaled terror. We tap grey throats of patrilineal beech-dolls for sap, smear beards and handlebar mustaches on father-photographs with half-truth grease, drink our bull's blood by crystal decanters then lengthily vomit woodchips of broken promises. In blue plastic barrels of bubbling apricot we breakdown like rainclouds and convert the sugar of our voices into acid. We inhale cimbalom-colostrum by silver dairy pails (for if we do not get the F MINOR KEY antibodies regularly, we will be defenseless against the F MINOR KEY)!

Amongst the dead-living womenfolk of my family, there is a pecking order of tears. Transparent pears of salt, sticky psychic nestlings cradled and warbling in the plates of a rigged set of balancing scales. An early adolescent descendant does not dare cry for being sodomized by her school abuser because her ancestor's child-son was killed when his foot detonated a landmine while she was being harassed by a soldier. A late adolescent descendant does not dare cry post-failed-suicide because her ancestor, whose father killed himself when she was a toddler, almost died eating rotting meat while hiding sugar in a padlás with her sister and mother. As a rule, the shadow of your ancestor's neglected grief must always fall full upon the surface of yours, prohibited! A medical mystery does not dare cry about dysfunctional organs dysfunctional glands because the xylem of one legally blind ancestor's spine is fungal with scarring lesions and another ancestor was a wheelchair user. As a rule, the shadow of your ancestor's somatic suffering must always fall full upon the surface of yours, fictional! My mother was a broken record: MIÉRT ITATOD AZ EGERE-KET? WHY ARE YOU GIVING DRINKS TO THE MICE? But here, my grandmother's laughter is lupine. But here, I am dated older than my great-grandmother by ring counting. I say REPEAT AFTER ME: WE WILL NO LONGER MAKE INVISIBLE RUNGS OF EACH OTHER'S TEARS! MAY OUR PRIVATE COLLECTIVE POOL OF TEARS BE A LADDER WE DO NOT CLIMB INTO CELESTIAL FEASTING BUT DISEMBARK INTO MYCORRHIZAL SOIL WHERE WE ACKNOWLEDGE THE GIFTS OF REFLECTION, REGULATION, RECONCILIATION.

KÜLDÖTT FARKAS, KIS KÍSÉRTETKUTYA, my grandmother shepherds me, in a tone of pastry, far beyond a river of silver knives like dead fish. I bend my face into the saline lake of her body. True, I have observed bad practices since a whelp pulling my umbilical leash, going father-picking four-legged in THE ORCHARD OF GOOD AND TRUE FATHERS, pretend picking my good and true father, a polished red apple (no poison!) I held fixed in my jaw, reabsorbing the humiliation of proteins. A Sapphic lavender-violet wreath upon my head, I was raised hungry, flea-hearted, hypoglycemic, often hairless in peach-sized patches, lapping up spiral galaxy breast milk in the rose-bloom wombs of my dreams, my urethra burning like vomit, my bladder diseased, inflamed, scarred, and popping, I was urine-marking everything, all ketones and albumin, leaving behind my very own feral scent so I could recognize myself later on, pawing at clots of false hope which hung from glistening butcher hooks like my favorite egg noodle dumplings. But here, I do raise myself all over and over again, and you, too, are my own daughters! Here, we no longer eat our own bark, wood, leaves, but turn our flower clusters into palacsinta.

SELF-PORTRAIT WITH FANGS

In my grandmother's inclement dreams, she began
grinding her teeth, bedwetting. An increase of acetylcholine:
sister-in-blood sisters-in-law became subterranean, ectothermic,
gnawing on roots & seedlings & sprouts
like a phlegm of garden
slugs. Her dead: invertebrates, blisters, tongues, rain-
risen, laying eggs. In the cellar, her mother's rage writhing
(terrestrial lateral undulation)
in salt. To keep it fresh,
I heard my great-grandmother preserved
the cup from which her husband poisoned himself
with photographic chemicals after border
changes & the violin
he disemboweled with a bow,
gushing the guts of rusting songs. An alimentary canal,
her rage is seven meters long stretched out. A garden hose,
from the house of her rage, my grandmother's rage
a water snake she was un-
snarling. My rage, pressurized vomit, cuspid
sharp. An animal I no longer want
to incubate. The truth:
I was going broody once, birthing untranslatable storms, pecking aggressively at
my own skin, raising up gooseflesh nests. It is in our story—displacement—to harm
ourselves by mistake in the absence of patriarchs making
half-orphans of suckling
litters, spitting out irradiated milk
from the snakebites of our mothers' breasts, this prescription
a myth, a dangerous myth. I was
never their whistle-disciplined girl. In my lineage,
girl is a title at which we let vultures pick, metabolize
in gastric battery acid. We are sanguivorous ghost-hounds sharing
a syrinx, so hungry not even ecliptic
noshing of plasmatic & satellitic celestial bodies can fill

our salival stomachs. In other words, we are
one third fork-tongued conspicuous song-
bird, one third BEYOND-THE-CORVUS order Chiroptera
with social microbiomes, one third phantom-branched mother-
without-mother-character, so far from
knowing the meaning of home, wings abscise feathers by resorption.
We become remige-translucent first,
thermoreceptors on our noses locating pulses
our friction-ridged fingers will never
reach, like waltz-time-light-speed.

Speleotherapy

And when our train reached Eger from Keleti Pályaudvar, I stuck my phantom molar back into my jaw like a tulip bulb. On the railway platform, DÉDNAGYBÁCSI's firstborn son T. whom my mother always spoke of like a beloved older brother, now wore my grandmother's delicate death-face. Yes!—The very same pear-shaped nose, pinched lips, socketed buccal region symmetrically rune-spelling V like a skein of migrating mute swans or wild geese.

V for   v   arránőm

                                        v   acog a foga

                        v   ándormadár

                                                    v   alameddig távolság

T.'s hands thatched together, fingers braided, he garlanded his own slightly distended abdomen like a cradle made of limbs; an endearing idiosyncrasy I would later anticipate on our daily excursions together. He was older now, slightly hunched yet substantial (not wind-vulnerable, for example). I last saw him four years before, here in Heves County. My grandmother's delicate death-face now slapped upon T.'s aging face turned my body immediately into a meadow of resurrection-fresh snow. His mulberry-haired wife, a history teacher, intelligent and profusely generous, shares a name with DÉDNAGYNÉNI on NAGYPAPA's side: in Magyar folklore, THE QUEEN OF THE DRAGON WOLVES.

THE QUEEN OF THE DRAGON WOLVES prepared for our afternoon together traditional herdsman stew with the inclusion of root vegetables. Scarlet droplets of lard lily-padded liquid's surface, which steamed like dragon's breath. EGRI MAMA, I.'s short white-hind-like mother, shepherded us toward her single tiny dining table draped in embroidery, which we all gathered around, shoulders touching, stew-slurping in summertime's July navel. Her living room wall wept a decorative fabric illustrating a quintet of skirted geometric women extending botanical organisms from their stick figure palms. Ceramic plate after ceramic plate star-webbing her kitchen wall like Horologium Oscillatorium. The old peacock ladle hung vertical in the center like an hour hand. The old ladle whose handle resembled a tavern-dancing bull's nose ring hung vertical close by, a complementary minute hand. EGRI MAMA's movements reminded me of my own grandmother's kitchen choreography. Triglycerides informed my blood—(My forrobinieaemothers materialized, bográcsozás or cauldron-cooking in EGRI MAMA's garden of botanical acrobats and wasp-worship . . . I had never before known wasp song one could likely record seismographically. Making music for a wasp is translating the body's stellar pulsations. Distance was emerald, proximity was emerald, I was unlearning gravity's grasp in July . . .) After immaculate apricot brandy and paprika-infused stew, we had Zserbó cake, pogácsa with caraway, and peach juice. I did not yet know how village dog song would soon drip from my earlobes like rain-silver jewelry.

Those collagenic needles of my forrobinieaemothers' still-decomposing bones sewed belated dragon-fire frequency in and out of volcanic slopes like our traditional textile fabric's red thread. In DÉDANYA ANNA's Northeastern howling garden, I was barefoot and burning deliciously with epiphany. Once, I told my mother that I do not know why I write compulsively for and toward our women while simultaneously, I emphatically resent the wound I have received from them; an unsolicited inheritance laced (in gradations of unintentionality) with viper venom. Her quick unscripted response: THE STORY CALLS YOU. To enter those stalactitic and stalagmitic Caves of Aggtelek Karst and Slovak Karst, particularly The Baradla-Domica cave system, one must first locate VÖRÖSTÓ or The Red Lake; an X MARKS-THE-SPOT. I call such cartographic information a metaphor for the practice of untangling complicated gnarls of transgenerational grief like brushing out knots in bat roost hair. First, one must discover the vermillion existence of it. Then, one must negotiate interstitial icicled corridors between a pendent past and an erupting future, and furthermore, consider how they touch each other and open homesick-wide and unslakable like reciprocal regurgitating beaks.

In the Room of Giants, NAGYPAPA's quintet of autoimmune sisters, who all rumoredly measured around six-foot-tall, provided me, acoustically, with prescient medicine. In the Hall of Tigers, I found NAGYMAMA and NAGYPAPA pendulating in borderlands. My mother learned that in Hungary—before 1957—if a woman citizen married a noncitizen, her citizenship was relinquished and no longer recognized. NAGYMAMA existed liminally between stalagmitic Hungary and stalactitic Czechoslovakia, and NAGYPAPA was a Transylvanian Hungarian—born and raised in Romania—who experienced language and education trauma, and who was grateful for his Romanian schoolteacher, a man who, in spite of prescribed divisions of nationalisms, treated NAGYPAPA like a son. I have family bones in Eastern European villages where languages are beautiful together. No family bones here but beloved dust of defectors.

WHERE, FOR YOU, IS HOME?

WHERE REVISIONIST WALL-BUILDING ÖRDÖGÖK WHITEWASH AND COLLAPSE HISTORY ...
PERPETUATING
HISTORICAL TRAUMA FOR POLITICAL GAINS?

(THE STORY CALLS YOU TO ENTER)

TO QUESTION

In the Room of Lace, dragon-fire frequency pierced through inscrutable reverie. Each rhyolitic reverie-gate I entered like a Hercegkút cellar, finding misplaced fabric artifact after misplaced fabric artifact, snacking on leftover Zserbó cake and a Hollohazi thimble like a stale cukor (plucked from NAGYMAMA's neverending purse!) made not only of grape but tulip, rose, lily, and pigeon.

The fossils of my great grandmother's extinct
upholstered székek unearthed right here.

—Distance, for some time.—

The spiderweblike scraps of my grandmother's (citizenship-
relinquishing) wedding dress snagging insects over there.

—O, my seamstress!—

The dust of my mother's bloody labor
gown blushing up here.

—Wandering bird.—

The ruins of my grief-given kitchen linen ant-hilling down there.

—Her teeth are chattering.—

ICA NÉNI was once DÉDANYA ANNA's closest neighbor. A seamstress resurrecting dresses! My mother helped mend when she—nine and completely alone by aircraft into Austria and subsequently by bus into Hungary (foreign wingéd things could not enter her home country then, my mother said, no plumaged aluminum-titanium cradles carrying second generation scaled children with wolf-bird selenic fur, heliac feathers)—visited DÉDANYA ANNA in the summers of her satellitic childhood. At dusk, my great-grandmother would tuck my mother snugly into her own cocoon of goosedown, whip házilegyek away from her bedroom and toward concrete-corridor-light with a tea towel, and leave a basin into which my mother would urinate in evening hours; afraid of venturing into DÉDANYA ANNA's dark outhouse (where spiders held moth-ensnaring dinner parties!) underneath a wolf-gnawed August moon. During chrysalid midnights in their shared cocoon, my mother's body would digest itself, holometabolous, and when she emerged rematerialized, she had ultraviolet sight. Now, ICA NÉNI lives vigorous-delicate and elegant in her domestic ferality amidst my great-grandmother's roosters, hens, and red currant bushes. In the Room of Lace, summoning silk spirits, ICA NÉNI incised, with her soil-rich fingernails, a line in limestone: BÁRMERRE VISZ SOR-SOM ÚTJA HAZA VÁGYOM CSENDES KIS FALUMBA meaning WHEREVER MY DESTINY TAKES ME I LONG TO GO HOME TO MY QUIET LITTLE VILLAGE. Hers never was.

(THE CALL TO YOU ENTERS STORY)

When I emerged like an inside-out butterfly after bodypacking myself into NAGYMAMA's crowning arboreal urn, my skull was briefly, fetally, shaped like a cauldron. I was salivating for language with which I could play hopscotch on the deceptive snail grid of death. Children began pointing and remarking on my appearance—I overheard TRIPLE RAINBOW. QUADRUPLE RAINBOW too. A poet casted her imperative: TELL ME WHAT YOU KNOW ABOUT DISMEMBERMENT.

1) Does a house have elliptical wings?

      2) Do roots & feathers ever reflect politicians' nationalisms, map lines, names?

      Aren't bodies more important than borders?

      THE PEOPLE ARE NOT YOUR PAWNS, THE PEOPLE ARE NEIGHBORS.

3) Who waters ghosts of houses like cornflowers tended by tender rain?

4) If I, without my grandmother like a shepherd & with my tongue not yet familiar, cannot ever truly go home, whose foundation is an alphabet in her hands, have I definitely lost my daughter character?

I was raised secondhand homesick by an oak-surrounded lake. Often, when I swam, I imagined I was being water-cradled by Lake Balaton's extensional tectonic embrace. After my failed suicide, I was banished like my great-grandfather; I became a bog ghost light with only rudimentary understanding of my language of grapevines, nock-draw-loosing at abstractions of home with minute hands. Only my grandmother welcomed me back, inviting me into the freshwater asylum of her thorax. My mother was raised on a river after a surgeon butchered my szerelő grandfather's spine during a surgical operation, forcing them further into poverty. I wonder if my mother ever imagined that her girlhood house was receiving a Danubian flood-transfusion whenever the structure's foundation filled, domestic belongings like organs molding from plasmatic precipitation, turning septic. And I wonder if, throughout all those years of flooding, my grandmother's tea kettle (like THE QUEEN's now) howled incessantly, porcelain-moon-desperate, a train horn cicada-decibeled in the grating key of vapor.

In New Jersey, when my mother is gasped back into the body of a daughter, I slowly loosen the sewing-kit-medicine-box of my grandmother's süti tin from a linen mountain in our pantry, extract chamomile exported from Great Plain salinity, boil a pot of tap water, and tip my mother's face over the mirror of the tea so that she may inhale the earth-apple-infused mist-billows like chord inversions.

Grand Daughter Blowing Dandelions

What I want is a scalloped sponge cake
        placed upon your tongue like a misplaced coin, nickel-plated.
The room of your last domestic slumber (your slumber without wind)
        hexagonal prismatic, preserved.
I want the nectar of your every meteoric slumber
        heretofore kept in a petaled locket around my neck unlike acceptance.
I do not want death's refractive fingers elastic castling your cupboards.
I do not want my mother scrambling solving the puzzles of your still-swarming drawers.
I do not want your gossamer sweaters ever digested in the washer's small intestine.
I want your stomach full of bread, not how you left us; loafless.
I want a symmetric egg timer whose viscera was formed from sand
        once crusted in the corners of your sunrise eyelids.
What I want, retrospectively, is a topographic map of your spider veins, plum-rich.
An aircraft could not take me wherever you are now, I would require a sárkány. I want a sárkány.
A ligament like a string phone connecting meadowed bone of the living
        to meadowed bone of the dead,
        at each end vadárvácskák like exoskeletons we hold our ears against.
I want adoration translated into recipe. As if unriddling a silver thicket of hair.
        To sustain myself with the poppy seed & custard cream of mother tongue.
        To wield the sunlit cutlery & stained linen of your cadence.
If only I had let the snow tinseling your scalp vanish like powdered sugar in my mouth.
If only I could shoo away a roosting word like VANISH fanged,
        hematophagous from my cerebral cortex.
        The taxonomy of NEVER—GEOSPIZA SEPTENTRIONALIS.
The taxonomy of NOWHERE—CALYPTRA THALICTRI.
I want your pastel yellow nightgown back. To rescind cremation.
To have become prophetic in December's embryonic phase.
To have orchestrated a forestial slumber party every dusk thereafter my vatic smack
        during which I would have breastfed you baracklé,
        rejuvenated your face with Hungarian thermal mud, paprika, cinnamon.
        Blown you—pigeons of kisses! Crows of kisses! Swallows of kisses!
Distance is so ridiculous. Distance is so celestial, so thistle.
What I want is a bird that reaches you in time.
What I want is time inverted like a navel.

Burying Porcelain Horses

Is hers a redundant hoofprint in this rampantness called death?—
stomping ribboned voltage, soil-angeling a halo,
a cauldron whose brothy overabundance
is simultaneously atmospheric & lachrymal.
To ladle salt by approximation into
the gnaw of unlocatable wounds.
Distance is stew-thick, trumpeting exquisite
temperatures. Her death unthatched
the private stable that once existed
between us like a hush. I walk now
amongst scattered sheaves of tenderness & wheat.
I was dream-wrecked for days enduring
the tinnitus of January light,
my body ablaze & in slumber not sensing
that NAGYMAMA had already swaddled herself
in her embroidered birkabőr coat
& begun her breadcrumbless departure back
toward daughterhood, pearls & silver coins petaling her clavicle.
Yet somehow my stomach understood. Prescient
dates blinking like bioluminescent insects inhabiting
my red poppy dream-plain understood.
I was forecasting numbers. I was rummaging for the very last words
I would never say—descended bird eggs. I will never
again say vörösmadár, gyulladás, hasonlatosság, gyógyíthatatlan.
A tourniquet for dormant telepathic correspondence (burning
silence) is doubtful. But didn't
the red stag visit me aglow & knowing?
I do not trust anything. I was not ready
for such bow-hunting & obliqueness & disbelief.
I am lost in the honeycomb of bird-watching
her apparition, I am viscous with
the glucose of agglutinative language,
dreaming suddenly in the thunderous

metal utensils of mother tongue, burying
porcelain horses in earth that could
not contain her.

Abban az irányban, éjszakai angyal akusztika.

Almáskertről álmodni újra és újra és újra.

Anélkül hogy egyetlen égető szót is kimondani, átúszni egy befagyott folyón.

A piroklasztikus ábécéjének fekete kapuja, nyisd ki.

Apránként: aludttej, alvadt vér, tükörszilánk, áramfeszültség, anyanyelv.

In that direction, nocturnal angel acoustics.

To dream of an apple orchard over and over and over.

To swim across a frozen river without saying a single burning word.

Dream of a river without direction. The black gate of her pyroclastic alphabet, open it.

Dream a tongue over a frozen word. Little by little: curdled milk, clotted blood, splintered mirror, current voltage, mother tongue.

To swim in the blood of her mother saying: a single burning angel.

To open, mother, swim in that dream of saying. I wish I could howl like a wolf.

She bit hungrily into her mother's ripe language, spilling nectar.

Bárcsak üvölthetnék mint egy farkas. Shivering on-blue-violet-fire: I wish I could heal my skin like the sky, I said.

Beleharapott éhesen majd anyja érett nyelvébe, kiömlő nektár.

Borzong kék-lila-tűzön: Bárcsak meggyógyíthatnám a bőrömet mint az eget, mondtam.

With sugar, dust her wound. I wish I could dream of a howl that could heal over.

Cukorral porozza be a sebét. Rosehip bush, let yourself cry unashamedly. I wish I could open like an orchard, like a sky.

Csipkebogyó bokor, hagyd magad sírni szégyen nélkül. I wish I could swim across the violet-black current of her alphabet.

My mother's wound open like a howl, I swim in it without direction. I wish I could mother that shivering river.

I wish I could mother her pyroclastic wound.

I wish I could heal the wolf of her wound with a river-blue dream.

In the orchard of her alphabet, unashamedly on fire, I cry like an angel.

In December, I am discordant like a bat's roost, like a hornet's nest.

In December, I am a chambered stomach growling thunderously like ghosts of cloister ruins.

Decemberben, olyan disszonáns vagyok mint a denevér odúja, mint a darázs fészke.

Decemberben, többkamrás gyomor vagyok amely mennydörgően morogva, mint kolostorromok szellemei.

I am little in the nest of her alphabet, spilling language like on-blue-violet-fire blood.

Let yourself cry, my mother, I said, over and over.

Let yourself cry, my mother's mother, I said over.

Ecetviharokat jósolok. I am little in the ruins of her wound, discordant like a wolf with a burning wish.

Egyszer egy egész nap égve hagyta a koordinátáit.

Elküldtem száz levelet. Megkaptad őket, vándormadaramat?

Elválaszthatatlanság illúziójának vége.

Engedetlenségem, megünnepeled? Engedetlenséged megmérgezte ásványi zenédet.

Erdei vadnak érzem magam. I predict vinegar storms.

I posted a hundred letters. Did you receive them, my wandering bird?

She once kept her coordinates lit all day.

The illusion of inseparability is gone.

My disobedience, are you celebrating it? Your obedience poisoned your mineral music.

I predict splintered music. I feel forest feral.

In the poisoned forest of my stomach, a growling angel in a rosehip cloister.

I feel like I am the blue sky spilling burning coordinates and burning letters all day.

The black forest of my mother's stomach is the black forest of her mother's stomach, in it, I am nocturnal and word-wandering.

Fecske belsejében: fáklya, fénytörés, hajfürt, szőlőfürt, filharmónia.

Figyelj, a torkom folyosóján egy fecskét ringatok.

Figyelj, félek hogy a félhold hamarosan viaszként megolvad.

Földieper fészkeket építek a fülemben az árnyékainknak.

Inside that swallow: torch, refraction of light, lock of hair, cluster of grapes, philharmonic.

Listen, I cradle a swallow in the corridor of my throat.

Listen, I am afraid that the crescent moon will soon melt like wax.

I am building strawberry nests in my ears for our shadows.

I am afraid of that feral angel wandering hungrily across the forest of my tongue.

Her frozen music will soon melt into my skin like a river of minerals. Galambforgalom van közöttünk.

I wish I could cradle my mother's philharmonic howl.   Gyűszűd nemzedékek könnycseppjeit gyűjti, mint egy porcelán bogrács.

I wish I could swallow the dust of her wound like sugar.   There is pigeon traffic between us.

Your thimble collects generations of teardrops like a porcelain cauldron.

I am building a porcelain corridor between the orchard of her alphabet and my wandering tongue.

She hungrily collects generations in the stomach of her wound.

There is a word between us like a poisoned apple. Postwar, she foamed at the mouth.

Háború után habzott a szája. There is a wish between us like an illusion.   If only I had left river fish bones in your village mailbox.

Hacsak folyami halcsontokat hagytam volna a falusi postaládájában.   If only I had known the medicine of fresh mountain air.

Hacsak tudtam volna a friss hegyi levegő gyógyszerét.   If only I had known the secret location of her silver bridge.

Hacsak tudtam volna az ezüst hídjának titkos helye.   It is snowing sound vibrations.

Havazik hangrezgések.   Homewards, I made a spelling mistake.

Hazafelé, helyesírási hibát vétettem.   I was moonlit. I was taciturn. Why?

Holdvilágos voltam. Hallgatag voltam. Miért?   If only I had generations shivering secret vibrations into my ears.

If only I had made a homewards bridge of light inside of a howl.

The moon of my stomach foamed silver at the mouth for the angel bones of language.

Postwar, my mother's mother left her mouth in a dream.

Igaz, hogy a mocsarak mellett virágzó íriszek jelenléted előhírnökei, itt-ott?

Is it true that the irises blooming by the bogs are harbingers of your presence, here and there?

Is it true that the silver-blue mountain collects generations of village ghosts?

Is it true that inside her frozen secret there is a roost of porcelain bones?

Is it true that a bridge is an illusion if here and there are in mirror ruins?

Her teardrops left bogs in the wound of my throat over and over and over.

Jövőben, a júniusi melegben, jácintból készült jászol egy kinyilatkoztatáshoz.

In the future, in the heat of June, a crib made of hyacinth for a revelation.

In June, I am shivering with the heat of her music.

In the future, her wound is a porcelain strawberry moon I howl at.

You are gone and I am spelling the word inseparability on my mother's skin with a blue hyacinth.

Kiszítta nap a hálóingedet.   You are gone and my mother is spilling ghosts like sugar.

Konyhakertjében a kiejtés koreográfiáját gyakoroltuk.

Koordinátarendszer mint egy kutyafalka, amely a koponyámon kopogtat. The sun faded your nightgown.

We practiced the choreography of pronunciation in her kitchen garden.

In her kitchen garden, a word is blooming like a stomach.   A coordinate system like a pack of dogs knocking against my skull.

In her kitchen garden, a stomach collects vibrations of faded light.

Unashamedly moonlit with disobedience, I practiced the medicine of teardrops.

Village dogs cry irises over a future you are gone in.

Your girlhood was a thick grove of air raid sirens.

Lánykorod légiszirénák vastag ligete volt.

Lehetetlen pillangó vagy, lyukas szárnyakkal. You are an impossible butterfly with perforated wings.

Lekéstem az utolsó vonatot hazafelé ezen jelenések labirintusában. I missed the last train in this labyrinth of apparitions.

In the stomach of December, I missed her last shivering word.

I missed her last shivering word like medicine.

Méhkas, kérlek taníts meg az otthon szent mézédes geometriájára.

Mit keresel itt, ahol a madár se jár?

My mother's mother's dream inside my mother's dream inside my dream is a kitchen fire inside of a chambered stomach inside of a labyrinth.

There, an angel in the cradle of a wolf is the heat saying: feel. Beehive, please teach me the sacred honeyed geometry of a home.

What are you doing here where the birds do not go?

What are you doing here in this mouth without coordinates?

What are you doing here, knocking on the lock of my wound?

A home is a geometry of acoustics, a home is a labyrinth of shadows, perforated sound, postwar light, porcelain ruins

The last crescent of her presence is a crib I listen in.

A library of dried plant specimens, her obituary.

Növénygyűjtemény listája, az Ő gyászjelentése. I say it unreservedly: your death's equinoctial overture was a rusted scissor.

Nyíltan kimondom: a halálod napéjegyenlőségi nyitánya rozsdás olló volt.

If it is snowing language, I am here in a garden of frozen letters, spelling angel with a scissor made of my shivering bones.

An angel is a library of wolf-birds that swallow the blood moon like fresh air. Operaház tartja a gyógyír retrográd amnéziájára.

The blood moon is a true torch wandering silver-black music. Öleld a kaolin, földpát, kvarc összetört örökségedet.

A rusted mouth is an open wound I do not heal. Őso öltéshez pókselyem szükséges.

The opera house holds the cure for her retrograde amnesia.

Embrace your shattered inheritance of kaolin, feldspar, quartz.

The ancestral stitch requires spider silk.

Her angel is a library of wolf-birds in our house blooming a hundred burning wings.

Her angel is a library of wolf-birds in our house with a philharmonic howl made of retrograde vibrations.

The cure for music shattered like a mirror is the blue silk stitch of a sacred ancestral river.

The cure for death's last direction is the refraction of a dream.

Pirkadatkor, padláson, madárdal ínszalagjai szöknek ki egy lánya szegycsontjából.

Pormentes gyomromban: postagalamb, a kristályprizma szirmok szivárványát szórja szét, pulzus mint egy transzgenerációs csók.

At dawn, in the attic, ligaments of birdsong escape from the sternum of a daughter.

In my dustless abdomen: a carrier pigeon, a crystal prism scattering a rainbow of petals, a pulse like a transgenerational kiss.

Régen itt egy ház állt, mint rejtekhely. In our home, a wound with a pulse collects.

Ritmikus rovarfrekvenciákat itt becsatornáztam a testembe itt. In our home, a wound where the birds do not go, it requires.

There used to be a house here like a hiding place. In our home, I did predict death's quartz and feldspar kiss.

I channeled rhythmic insect frequencies into my body here. In our home, a daughter is a cure, known.

What equinoctial dream am I in like a mirror scattering ligaments of silver-black music-light?

There used to be a pulse knocking inside my ears here rhythmic in this house.

There used to be heat here in the torch of my taciturn mouth inside this house.

Sehonnan vagyok. There used to be a body to be here in the daughter where the storms go inside this house.

Szájról szájra, mi a száműzetés aritmetikája? I am from nowhere.

Személyazonosságát igazolja, ez a sebhely. It proves her identity, this scar.

Szótagokat dobálok minden irányban, mint a sót, mint a szerveket. What is the arithmetic of exile, from mouth to mouth?

I throw syllables like salt like organs in all directions.

Táncolok a tövisek és tücskök temetőjében.
Tárcsázom a harmonikát amely talajban dobog.
Térképjelek, megeszem őket.
Termálvíz, ki vagyok száradva érte.
Tükörképem többes szám.
Tyúkólban, távbeszélő helyett egy talány találtam.

Utána, csak ujjlenyomatok.
Üvegházban ükanyám újra virágzik.
After, only fingerprints.
In a glasshouse, my great-great-grandmother is growing again.

I dance in her graveyard of thorns and crickets.
I dial the accordion beating in the soil.
Map symbols, I eat them.
Thermal water, I am parched for it.
My reflection is plural.
In the henhouse, instead of a telephone, I found a riddle.

I am from the on-blue-violet-fire crescent of her scar.
I eat a hundred syllables, her syllables made of petals and thorns.
I eat a hundred teardrops, her teardrops made of sugar and salt.
My reflection, it is impossible arithmetic, listen.

Véreb, hol volt hol nem volt.
Vidéki nő, hol volt hol nem volt.
Vonósnégyes, hol volt hol nem volt.
A bloodhound, once upon a time.
A countrywoman, once upon a time.
A string quartet, once upon a time.

After, her tongue dried over, tongue of dust, tongue of soil.
To pack my wound spilling birds clotted, she used her kiss of kaolin.
In the mirror a wolf is an after hiding in the body of a daughter.
In the mirror a wolf is an after growing in the body of a daughter.

Once upon heat, my grandmother left her mouth in the nowhere of a thermal water dream cluster.
Once upon direction, death's bloodhound did escape the rosehip labyrinth kept inside the burning map of my mother's abdomen.
It is snowing the letters of her alphabet like petals that melt upon my tongue again, again, again.
Time is an illusion inside of an illusion inside of an illusion.

Once upon a time, my body was a kept-secret graveyard of shattered after-light.
Once upon a time, my body was a scattering of pyroclastic birds, wings beating the soil of the sky.
Her last correspondence like a revelation was a scissor and a string.
If only I had known that a daughter, her body, is not an in between.

Wattnyi levelezést.
A watt of correspondence.
X-szer-mondtam-már.
I told you X times.

Zenetörténete egy zivatar.
Zsarátnok vagy.
The history of music is a thunderstorm.
You are live coals.

A mother will eat the howl of her daughter like it is a true cure.
Why did you mistake the wolf growing plural in my reflection for a rainbow?
I told you a hundred times, you did throw your wish like a crystal into the cauldron of my skull and I did embrace it like dawn.
I told you a hundred times, my body was a house in a dream where I let your accordion of apparitions go.

The history of a daughter is building a home with a beating pulse a hundred times over for fire to dance shadows like spelling.
The history of a daughter is growing a garden of blood for a wound with a stomach of air that will swallow time like a mirror.
I stitch the butterfly of my sternum to scar with a string of fingerprints after spilling a cry from throat to throat to throat.
The coals of language are lit like organs all across my body where the storms go after burning for growing over, growing over and over again.

NOTES

"THE SHAPE OF MY BODY IS DUST" was inspired by Hala Alyan's "Interactive :: House Saints."

The right-aligned lines in "Snowfield" are from Sir Walter Scott's "THE LADY OF THE LAKE (HYMN TO THE VIRGIN)," which Franz Schubert originally composed "Ave Maria" for.

A line in "Howler Tone" is from Venus Khoury-Ghata's "WORDS," in *Alphabets of Sand*.

The names of enamel rod end patterns in "Ameloglyphics" are from "AMELOGLYPHICS: THE TOOTH SIGNATURE" in *Oral and Maxillofacial Pathology Journal*, published July–December 2018.

In "MOLTING IN THE MÁTRA MOUNTAINS," "Until You Are Young" was a phrase my grandmother habitually vocalized, scrambling conjunctions in English, her second language. She meant something like: live, truly live while you are still young, but she accidentally and unknowingly replaced "while" with "until." To make an accurate phrase with until, it would be something like: live, live until you are dead. I never corrected her. This phrase was bewildering for me; a semantic rupture in temporality, a confluence of present and future.

In "Dress Resurrection," some of the anatomical particulars of the pike perch-turned-dragon are inspired by Hungarian folk beliefs about the sárkány, which I found in Tekla Dömötör's *Hungarian Folk Beliefs*, published by Indiana University Press.

The "fear" repetitions and the János Kadár quotation in "GOOSEFLESH" are from James P. Niessen's "HUNGARIAN REFUGEES OF 1956: FROM THE BORDER TO AUSTRIA, CAMP KILMER, AND ELSEWHERE."

For Piroska, I pulled information about the ancient custom of egg decoration from "HUNGARIAN EASTER EGGS" by Andy Meszaros on the Cleveland Hungarian Museum website.

"THE HEALER COUNTS BACKWARDS" is after what I call TEN MAGGOTS IN MY

ANIMAL, a Magyar folkloric curative incantation for banishing disease. Tekla Dömötör writes in *Hungarian Folk Beliefs*, "ACCORDING TO IMITATIVE MAGIC, AS THE LOWER NUMBERS ARE REACHED THE WORMS SHOULD DISAPPEAR FROM THE ANIMAL."

The phrase "lengthily vomits woodchips" in "Butcher Shop Rendezvous" is from Vénus Khoury-Ghata's "Widow" in *Alphabets of Sand*.

The line "COLLAPSE HISTORY . . . PERPETUATING HISTORICAL TRAUMA FOR POLITICAL GAINS" in "Speleotherapy" is directly from "Memory Politics in an Illiberal Regime" by László Szabolcs in *Public Seminar*.

The imperative in "Speleotherapy," "TELL ME WHAT YOU KNOW ABOUT DISMEMBERMENT," is from Bhanu Kapil's *The Vertical Interrogation of Strangers*.

"Grand Daughter Blowing Dandelions" was inspired by Mónica Gomery's "Granddaughter Casting Afternoon Shadows."

ACKNOWLEDGEMENTS

"Gingerbread" was originally published under a different title in *Diode Poetry Journal*.

"THE SHAPE OF MY BODY IS DUST" was originally published in *Hayden's Ferry Review*'s *Tiny Architectures*.

"Estefelé / Toward Evening" was originally published in Tupelo Press's *Milkweed Anthology*.

"Death Rattle Aubade" was a finalist for *Quarterly West*'s Annual Poetry Contest in 2022 and first housed in Issue 108.

"Piroska (Little Red Riding Hood)" is also housed in *Fairy Tale Review*.

"THE HEALER COUNTS BACKWARDS" was originally published in *Driftwood Press*.

"SELF-PORTRAIT WITH FANGS" was originally published in *Diode Poetry Journal*.

"Burying Porcelain Horses" was originally published in Bennington Review.

"THE HISTORY OF A DAUGHTER IS BUILDING A HOME WITH A BEATING PULSE / THE HISTORY OF A DAUGHTER IS GROWING A GARDEN OF BLOOD" was first housed in *A Velvet Giant* Issue 10.

Thank you Stephanie Choi, editor of *Quarterly West*, especially for your intentionality, support, and celebration.

To my teachers at Cornell University. To Valzhyna Mort for recognizing my voice, for the rain-fresh magic of defamiliarizing verbs, for your humorous guidance, and for teaching Anne Carson's "catastrophization" in your translation course. To Lyrae Van Clief-Stefanon for bewildering me with the rich music of your knowing, for encouraging my visceral listening, for forest workshops and waterside wanderings and our shared obsession with birds, and for teaching bonds, June Jordan's shimmering, and playing above the escapement in your trauma and invention course.

India Sada, there was no medicine in Ithaca like making you belly laugh until tears, and our long melting embraces. I have learned deeply from your heart and your stories. From your brilliant visions, intuitive experiments, and holistic practices in craft. Your sonorous wisdom like songs of water. Thank you for teaching me about nourishment. I love you very much. Mackenzie Berry, I never stop being inspired by your strength, your resilience, your vast and verdant and vibrant imagination. You are rooted and soulful and earthy and whenever you smiled in Ithaca, I felt like everything could be okay. I love you very much. I would not get lost in a labyrinthine forest under a red sky after midnight for hours with anyone else but you two. Thank you both for holding me up and helping me into the health center and hospital when I lost sensation in my legs during office hours. I am not sure if words could reach and touch my gratitude. Michael Lee, thank you so much for sharing your cottage with us, for opening up your home often so we could so intimately gather and collaborate in love, creativity, and flavorful stew (you even incorporated lavender!). Thank you for bringing warm lamplight when working together at Epoch. Bumping into you in the hallways of Goldwin Smith grounded me when I felt otherwise buoyant and atmospheric and untethered after my grandmother's death and during my medical crisis. I gained an abundance of necessary insight from your poetic (therefore political) meditations and interrogations. I love you very much. My gratitude for you all is tremendous. Writing beside you was an honor and a privilege. I know a better world is possible because of you. Thank you cohort familiars: Levis for your snuggles during a time of touch deprivation, August for trusting me and for all of our flirt pole fun, Luna for making my sides split with laughter at every single cigarette you tried consuming off the ground whenever we walked (I never let you!). Appa has joined the coolest cohort familiar community ever. To Appa, my dog son, for teaching me truest patience and for being my shadow.

To my mother, we mend beyond banishment, we will mend and mend, may we foil intergenerational curses together going forward. Thank you for your persistent reassurance that our language is, in fact, mine in spite of lack of fluency. It was the music of my living in your body. During Nana's last month that December, I felt I was your sister in tending her, shepherding her through hospice, and maintaining her dignity in death. Whenever you tell people your daughter is a writer, you mention how I was profoundly preoccupied with words since birth and that I would, like a broken record, implore you for synonyms until you got me thesauri and dictionaries and stories, within which I immersed myself and never really surfaced. Thank you for books! I love you. To my brothers, thank you for reading my chapters and asking about my characters even though you tease me. I will teach you our language. I love you. To my father, despite so much estrangement, I will always call. Thank you for believing me when I said I was ill and sending me research about post-viral fatigue, dysautonomia, disease, and symptoms across multiple organ systems. Most people made me feel hysterical but you did not. You show up in your ways and I love you. To Demetri, no matter what shape our relationship takes, ours is the knot that cannot be undone. Thank you for the dwelling place of your love. To Jack, thank you for bringing me back from my suicide attempt and for helping me develop a language for my trauma. I am alive because of you and our evening chess games.

To Csilla, for your generosity and your gulyás. To Tibor for your pálinka and for being like a brother for my mother. I love you both dearly. To Katinka, who collaborated with me in revising my translation projects, particularly "THE HISTORY OF A DAUGHTER IS BUILDING A HOME WITH A BEATING PULSE / THE HISTORY OF A DAUGHTER IS GROWING A GARDEN OF BLOOD." Thank you. I love you, my sister-cousin. To Lilo, for your art. For your painting, *MEET ME ON THE OTHER SIDE,* the beautiful cover of my book. Thank you. I love you, my sister-cousin.

To my teachers at William Paterson University: Timothy Liu, Christopher Salerno, and Martha Witt for your sustained support. To Eros Livieratos! Thank you for inspiring me with your beautiful work since the very beginning. I would not have applied for graduate school if it were not for you. I am so grateful we enrolled together in that graduate workshop our senior year. May we always be in community together making art and meaning.

To all the good ancestresses who call me. From Donegal to Cork, from Borsod-Abaúj-Zemplén to Transylvania.

To my Nagypapa László: I never met you but my mother says you raged against injustice. I love dogs like you and I think I have your heart. I promise I will grow yellow roses and leave offerings of chocolate at your urn.

To Ishion, thank you from the grove of my heart for finding love in this story.

Lastly, my Nagymama, életem, életem, életem:

Mom was a single parent working multiple jobs, so you welcomed us home from school, grade after grade, with paprikás csirke, nokedli, lecsó, húsleves, túrós csusza, édes tészta dióval, and more. In December, we made töltött káposzta and mákos beigli together. You served history lessons like potatoes. These memories with you are my home. The kitchen with you in it was my country. My only country. Thank you for teaching me sentences and numbers in Hungarian when we hung out in your bedroom, snacking on dried apricots and madeleines and chocolate. Thank you for sharing your girlhood with me. Thank you for letting me record your stories. Thank you for never abandoning me. Thank you for letting me pour your sugar and butter your bread. To tend you at the very end was the ultimate sacred privilege. I wish you had waited for me when you took your last breath so I could have sent you off like a mother when your mother finally came for you sometime between midnight and six in the morning. That I was sleeping when you left will always haunt me but I understand your need for privacy. Find me here and there and there and here and I will, in return, tell you all of my own stories.